American Expressions

AMERICAN EXPRESSIONS

A Thesaurus of Effective and Colorful Speech

Edited by
ROBERT B. COSTELLO

Consulting Editor
JESS STEIN

A Sachem / Norback Book

McGraw-Hill Book Company

New York St. Louis San Francisco Hamburg
London Mexico Sydney Toronto

1 2 3 4 5 6 7 8 9   DO DO   8 7 6 5 4 3 2 1

Library of Congress Cataloging in Publication Data

Main entry under title:
American expressions.
"A Sachem/Norback book."
1. English language—Terms and phrases.
2. Americanisms. 3. Figures of speech.
I. Costello, Robert B. II. Stein, Jess M.
PE2839.A45   423′.1   81-6030
ISBN 0-07-047137-1   AACR2

Contents

v

Behavior 39

Communication 49

Duty 57

Emotion 61

Mental World 77

Morality 87

Physical World 97

Quality *115*

Index

Preface

Colorful expressions are the spice of language. Without them, English would be greatly impoverished and much less effective. Clarity in the presentation of ideas or the description of people and events is essential, but it is generally not enough. It is colorful expression that brings things to life, that conveys feeling, and that heightens persuasiveness.

American English is particularly rich in colorful words and phrases, partly because of the large size of the language's vocabulary and partly because Americans are not afraid of change or experiment in language. We enjoy picturesque phrases; they may be colorful, humorous, ironic, fanciful, blunt, nasty, vulgar—but they are, above all, expressive and creative.

Colorful language takes many different forms. Sometimes it is created by exaggeration ("make a mountain out of a molehill") and sometimes by understatement ("get up on the wrong side of the bed"); sometimes it is simply a clever repetition of sounds ("fuss and feathers"); sometimes it is a metaphor or a simile or some other figure of speech ("scrape the bottom of the barrel").

The right expression can make the difference between a dull, pedestrian statement and a memorable, incisive one. Thus, during the Cuban missile crisis, Secretary of State Dean Rusk might have said, "We are in a dangerous confrontation but there is some indication that the other side may yield." Instead, he said with matchless color, "We're eyeball to eyeball, and I think the other fellow just blinked."

American Expressions is a thesaurus devoted specifically to a large selection of words and phrases in English that convey meanings greater than the sum of their parts. Some of the phrases recorded in this book have become so fixed in the language as to constitute clichés, yet their very persistence and familiarity testify to their usefulness. All those who seek greater effectiveness in their speech and writing—executives, teachers, students, writers, editors, broadcasters, and many others—will welcome this collection. It will prove useful and convenient, interesting and entertaining.

Many readers will have pet phrases and expressions that they think are as effective as those in *American Expressions.* The editors will welcome suggestions for future editions.

Action

Abandonment

give up the ghost
give up the ship
jump ship
leave flat
leave high and dry
leave holding the bag
leave holding the sack
leave in the lurch
let go hang

Ability

have something on the ball
have what it takes
know one's business
know one's onions
know one's stuff
know one's way around

know the ropes
know the score
sure-handed

Accomplishment

all in a day's work
bang-up job
do credit to
do one proud
do justice
feather in one's cap
follow through
get out from under
get someplace
get to first base
half the battle
make good
make hay
make hay while the sun shines
make it

1

make something of oneself
one down and two to go
out of the way
sew up

Acquisition

get one's hands on
latch on to
lay one's hands on
pick up
rack up
snap up

Activity

alive with
comings and goings
fuss and feathers
get around
go great guns
have one's hands full
hit the deck
high gear
in circulation
in full swing
live one
live wire
on the go
on the jump

Advantage

born with a silver spoon in
    one's mouth
foot in the door
have an edge on
have something going for one
have the jump on
have the knock on
head start
in pocket
in the catbird seat
inside track
lead a charmed life
money in the bank
put in a good word for
ride the gravy train
running start
sitting pretty
steal a march

Aggressiveness

boardinghouse reach
drive a hard bargain
drive to the wall
full steam ahead
give 'em hell
give the old one-two
go for the brass ring
go-getter
make bold
mouth off
move in on

Agitation

fuss and feathers
hot and bothered
hot and heavy
hot under the collar
in a dither
in a lather
in a spin
in a tailspin
much ado about nothing
steamed up
stir up
storm and stress
Sturm und Drang

Alertness

all ears
bright-eyed and bushy-tailed
clear-eyed
come alive
come to
come to life
come to one's senses
ear to the ground
eyes in the back of one's head
fast on one's feet
fast on the draw
get wise
get with it
have an eye out
Johnny-on-the-spot
keep a sharp eye out

keep a watchful eye
keep a weather eye open
keep an ear to the ground
keep an eye on
keep one's ears open
keep one's eye on the ball
keep one's eyes open
keep one's eyes peeled
keep one's eyes skinned
keep one's wits about one
keep pace
keep step
keep tabs on
keep track
look alive
look out
look sharp
no flies on
on guard
on one's mettle
on one's toes
on the alert
on the ball
on the qui vive
on the watch
on tiptoe
open-eyed
pick up on
quick-witted
sit up and take notice
switched-on

Ambition

climb the ladder of success
on the make
scale the heights

Animation

alive with
come alive
sign of life

Appearance

come off
come out
come to light
enter into the picture
heave into sight
heave into view
make an appearance
pop up
see the light of day
show one's face
show up
speak of the devil
speak of the devil and he
   appears

Anticipation

count one's chickens before
   they're hatched
cross a bridge before one
   comes to it
cross one's fingers
crow before one is out of the
   woods
cry before one is hurt
jump the gun
jump to conclusions
leap to conclusions
on pins and needles
on the edge of one's chair
on the edge of one's seat

Attack

fly at one's throat
fly in the teeth of
go at
have at
jump all over
jump down one's throat
jump on
jump on one's case
lace into
land all over
land on
lash out
lay a finger on
lay about one

lay into
lay on
let have it
let have it with both barrels
light into
open fire
open up
pitch into
rip apart
rip into
rip up
rip up one side and down the
    other
set on

hang on every word
lend an ear
listen up
on the qui vive
prick up one's ears
see after
see to

Attention

catch one's eye
get the eye
get the high sign
give one the eye
give the glad eye
give the high sign
make one sit up and take
    notice
mark well
point out

Attentiveness

all ears
give an ear

Attraction

catch one's eye
come-on
get the eye
good box office

Basis

at heart
bred-in-the-bone
dyed-in-the-wool
in substance
meat-and-potatoes
nitty-gritty
nuts and bolts
pure and simple
rock bottom

Causation

bring to pass
chain reaction
give rise to
on account of

Caution

a bird in the hand is worth two
    in the bush
a burnt child dreads the fire
a little knowledge is a
    dangerous thing
curiosity killed the cat
discretion is the better part of
    valor
haste makes waste
have a care
give the high sign
keep a watchful eye
keep a weather eye
keep an eye on
keep one's powder dry
little pitchers have big ears
look to one's laurels
on guard
once bitten, twice shy
people who live in glass
    houses shouldn't throw
    stones

Certainty

as sure as shooting
bet your boots
bet your bottom dollar
bet your hat
bet your life
bet your sweet life
beyond question
bottom dollar
by no means
for sure
lightning never strikes twice in
    the same place
make book
make sure
mark one's words
nail down
no doubt
no two ways about it
no way
no wonder
not by a damned sight
not by a jugful
not by a long sight
not by any means
not by any stretch of the
    imagination
not for the world
not for worlds
not on your life
not on your tintype
nothing if not
of course
open-and-shut
out of the question
pin down
rain or shine

shoo-in
slow but sure
slowly but surely
sure enough
sure thing
sure-fire
to be sure

Chance

by chance
by some miracle
finders keepers
finders keepers, losers
   weepers
in luck
tossup

Challenge

hard put
hard put to it
hard row to hoe
hard sledding
have a time
have one's work cut out for
   one
heavy weather
hell and high water
hell on wheels
hell or high water
in spite of
in the face of
in the teeth of
like looking for a needle in a
   haystack
like pulling teeth
rough sledding
run for one's money
run the gauntlet
sporting blood
take up the cudgels

Change

come a long way
come around
dance to another tune
rite of passage

Circulation

make the rounds
take the stump
take to the stump

Collapse

break down
break up
come apart at the seams
fall apart
give out

Control

get the tiger by the tail
have a finger in the pie
have a hand in
in charge
in one's court
in one's hands
in one's pocket
in the driver's seat
in the saddle
judgment seat
keep one's head
on top of
on top of things
psych out
pull strings
pull wires
push one's buttons
ride herd on
sew up
take charge
take hold
take over
turn around one's little finger
twist around one's little finger

under one's thumb
wrap around one's little finger

Courage

brave it out
brazen it out
chin up
get one's spunk up
get up gumption
get up nerve
get up on one's hind legs
have the courage of one's
    convictions
keep one's chin up
keep one's spirits up
pluck up one's courage
pure grit
tough it out
whistle in the dark

Crisis

at one's wit's end
at one's wits' end
grasp at straws
hit the panic button
in the clutch
moment of truth
life-and-death

life-or-death
point of no return
push the panic button
touch and go
when the chips are down
zero hour

Currying of Favor

apple polish
cozy up
get on one's good side
keep on the good side of
play up to
polish the apple
shine up to
suck around
suck up to

Decision

come to a crossroads
fish or cut bait
make up one's mind
shape up or ship out

Defeat

body blow
brick wall
bring down
bring down around one's ears
bring to one's knees
close up shop
come down
come down in the world
come to naught
comedown
cook one's goose
cry uncle
down for the count
down on one's luck
down-and-out
fall by the wayside
give in
in vain
kiss the canvas
meet one's Waterloo
mop the floor with
plow under
pull down
pull down from one's pedestal
pull one's teeth
take it on the chin
take the count
take the starch out of
take the wind out of one's sails
throw down
throw for a loop
throw for a loss
vote down
washed up
wipe out
wipe the floor with
wipe the ground with

Delay

drag one's feet
drag one's heels
give a rain check
hang fire
have lead in one's pants
sit on one's hands
stall for time
string out

Desperation

beg, borrow, or steal
between a rock and a hard
   place
clutch at straws
come hell or high water
drive to the wall
drive up the wall
for dear life
hit the panic button
on one's knees
scrape the bottom of the
   barrel
up a stump
up a tree
up against the wall
up the creek
up the creek without a paddle

Determination

come hell or high water
come what may
do-or-die
hell bent
hell bent for breakfast
hell bent for leather
hell-for-leather
hold one's ground
knock-down-and-drag-out
knock-down-drag-out
nail one's colors to the mast
never say die
now or never
on purpose
put one's foot down
roll up one's sleeves
screw up one's courage
see to it
set one's cap for
set one's face against
set one's heart on
set one's sights on
speak one's piece
square one's shoulders
stake a claim
take the bit in one's mouth
take the bit in one's teeth
take the bull by the horns
take the tiger by the tail
tough-minded

Discovery

blaze a trail
break ground
break new ground
bring to light
catch flatfooted
catch red-handed
catch with one's pants down
come across
come to light   ·
find out about
game is up
happen upon
hit upon
lay one's finger on
light upon

go sit on a tack
laugh off
lay aside
put out to pasture
send packing
send to the showers
show one the door
shrug away
shrug off
shut the door on
so much for
walking orders
walking papers
walking ticket
write off

Dismissal

get the air
get the ax
get the bum's rush
get the gate
get the old heave-ho
get the pack
give the brush-off
give the cold shoulder
give the sack
go chase oneself
go fly a kite
go jump in the lake
go peddle one's papers
go peddle one's wares

Disputation/ Disputatiousness

bone of contention
bone to pick
cross swords
crow to pick
free-for-all
hell you say
in dispute
last word
matter of opinion
on the contrary
take exception
take issue

Domination

bring to heel
call the shots
call the tune
call to account
clip one's wings
crack the whip
cut down to size
high-handed
hold all the cards
hold center stage
hold court
hold the stage
in charge
lay down the law
lead around by the nose
pull rank
push around
put in one's place
rule the roost
step all over
take center stage
wear the pants
wear the trousers

Duress

by the skin of one's teeth
hang by a hair
hang by a thread
in a bind
in a box

Dynamic Personality

ball of fire
hot number
hot one

Eagerness

ants in one's pants
fall all over oneself
fall over backwards
go great guns
not let any grass grow under
  one's feet

Economy

cut corners
cut to the bone
easy on the pocketbook
easy on the purse

Efficiency/ Effectiveness

do double duty
do the trick
go off like clockwork
hit on all cylinders
hit one's stride
kill two birds with one stone
time-tested
turn the trick

Effort

break one's neck
break through
by fits and starts
by the bootstraps
by the sweat of one's brow
fall over backwards
for all one is worth
give it all one's got
give one's all
go out of one's way
get out of one's way
go to the trouble
hammer out
have a go at
in there pitching
keep the ball rolling
lay to
lick into shape
lift a finger
make a pass at

might and main
move heaven and earth
muddle through
once over lightly
overachiever
peg away
pick-and-shovel
put one's back to
put one's best foot forward
put one's hand to
put one's hand to the plow
put one's nose to the
    grindstone
put one's shoulder to the
    wheel
see one's way clear to
set one's hand to
set one's hand to the plow
shoot at
shoot for
shoot the works
take pains
take the trouble
try one's hand
turn one's hand to
work like a beaver
work like a slave
work one's fingers to the bone
work on

Effortlessness

as easy as ABC
as easy as pie
breeze by
breeze through

Encounter

bump into
come face to face with
come to grips
cross swords
get one's teeth into
run across
run into
run upon
sink one's teeth into

Endurance

bear one's cross
bite the bullet
brave it out
can't hack it
carry a cross
cut it
cut the mustard
enough is enough
go the distance
go the limit
go the route
go through
hang in
hang in there
hang on
have a cross to bear
keep a stiff upper lip
keep pace
keep the home fires burning
last out

live down
live out
make the best of
patience of a saint
patience of Job
ride out
ride out the storm
roll with the punches
rough it
stand the gaff
stay the course
stay the round
stay with
staying power
stick it out
stick with it
survival of the fittest
sweat out
take it
until the last gun is fired
wear well
weather the storm

Energy

full of beans
full of fun
full of hops
full of Moxie
full of prunes
full of mischief
full of the devil
full of the Old Nick
full steam ahead
get up and go

get up nerve
get up one's gumption
hit the ground running
oomph
pep up
pepper-upper
perk up
pick-me-up
rolling stone gathers no moss
roll up one's sleeves
rough and ready
rough and tumble
shift into high gear

Enticement

come-on
rope into
siren's song

Escape

get while the going is good
go while the going's good
head for the hills
head for the woods
run away
run for it
skip out
slip through one's fingers
take a runout powder
take it on the lam
worm out of

Enjoyment

carpe diem
have a ball
hit the high spots
live a little
live it up
live to the full
make a day of it
make a night of it
make merry
nice as can be
out on the town
paint the town
paint the town red
primrose path
see the sights
seize the day
step out
step out on the town
three-ring circus
time of one's life

Eviction

boot out

Exhaustiveness

blow by blow
fine-tooth comb

Expedience

let's not and say we did
let's pretend

Firmness

hard as nails
hard nut to crack
hard-and-fast
hard-bitten
hard-boiled
hard-hitting
hard-nosed
hold one's ground
hold one's own
hold out
hold the fort
hold the line
stand by one's guns
stand one's ground
stand up for
stick to one's guns
stick up for
stiff as a board
strong-minded

Flight

beat a retreat
take to one's heels
take to the woods
turn tail

Forcibleness/ Forcefulness

bulldoze
by storm
like Dewey took Manila
like Grant took Richmond
strong-arm
strong-arm tactics

Fresh Start

clean bill of health
clean slate
clean up one's act
clear the air
get back to basics
make a new man of
make a new person of
make a new woman of
new blood
new broom sweeps clean
new lease on life

new wine in old bottles
second breath
second wind
shift gears
turn over a new leaf
wipe the slate clean

Frustration

beat one's head against a
   brick wall
beat one's head against a wall
blind alley
brick wall
climb the wall
have one's hands tied
hurry up and wait
run afoul of
sick to death of
tear one's hair

Fulfillment

come up in the world
come up to expectations
come up to snuff
make good
make the grade

Functionalism

all systems go
bridge the gap
chain reaction
do the trick
in force
in practice
in the running
of service
put to use

Futility

cast pearls before swine
draw a blank
go nowhere fast
rob Peter to pay Paul
save one's breath

Harassment

give a hard time
give one the needle
give the business
jump on one's case
on one's back
pick on
play cat and mouse with
start in on

Incitement

build a fire under
dangle a carrot in front of
   one's nose
egg on
light a fire under

Initiation

break in
break the ice
break through
cut one's eyeteeth on
get one's feet wet
show one the ropes

Inclination/Urge

have a mind
have an itch
have half a mind
have half a notion

Initiative

eager beaver
early bird catches the worm
let no grass grow under one's
   feet
of one's own accord
take the bit in one's mouth
take the bit in one's teeth
take the bull by the horns
take the tiger by the tail

Influence

cut no ice
prevail upon
pull strings
pull wires
push one's buttons
swing one's weight
throw one's weight around
turn one's head

Innovation

blaze a trail
break ground
break new ground

Interruption/ Interference

butt in
cramp one's style
crash the gate
fool around with
get a word in
get a word in edgeways
get a word in edgewise
gum up the works
have no business
horn in
in one's hair
in one's way
make waves
mess around with
mess over
monkey around with
muck about
muscle in
poke one's nose into
put in one's two cents worth
put in one's way
put in the way of
put the whammy
red tape
rock the boat
stand in the way of
step in
step on one's toes
stick one's nose into
tamper with
throw a monkey wrench into
thumb in the eye
tread on one's toes
upset the applecart

Manipulation

play off both ends against the middle
play off both sides against the middle
play one's cards right
play one's cards well
play politics
play the waiting game

Mastery

call the shots
call the tune
clamp down
clip one's wings
get the tiger by the tail

Means

by dint of
by hook or by crook

Opportunity/ Opportunism

brass ring
gravy train
have one's say
jump at the chance
jump on the bandwagon
make the most of
seize the day
strike while the iron is hot
take advantage of
time is ripe

Option

by choice
come to a crossroads
hand-pick
if the mountain won't come to
    Muhammad...
if worse comes to worst
name one's poison
take it or leave it

Opposition

fly in the face of
stand off
stand pat
stand up against
stand up and be counted
stand up to
stave off
stem the tide
swim against the current
swim against the stream
turn back

Outmaneuver

beat the gun
beat the system
beat to the draw
beat to the punch

Overcome

blow one's mind
boggle the mind
bowl over
cut a swath
knock in the aisles
knock into a cocked hat
knock off one's feet
knocked out
lay in the aisles

mind-bending
mind-blowing
out of sight
send into orbit
snow under
something else
sweep off one's feet
take by storm
take one's breath away

Panacea

bridge over troubled waters

Participation

along for the ride
do the honors
fall to
get on the bandwagon
go along for the ride
go in for
go out for
have a finger in the pie
have a hand in
help oneself
hold one's end up
in at the kill
in circulation
in for the kill
in the running

in the swim
in there pitching
jump in
jump on the bandwagon
keep one's hand in
kick in
listen in
make the scene
pitch in
pull one's own weight
put in one's oar
put in one's two cents
put in one's two cents' worth
sign up
sit in
stay in the running
take part
throw one's hat in the ring
time in
toss one's hat in the ring
weigh in

Persistence/ Perseverance

carry a torch
carry the torch
follow through
foot in the door
from way back
get after
go on
hold good
hold on
hold one's breath

hold over
hold true
keep after
keep at it
keep on trucking
keep one's nose to the
    grindstone
keep to
keep up
see through
stick to it
stick-to-itiveness
till death do us part
till the last gun is fired
tough it out
wear on

Possession/ Possessiveness

have an eye on
have dibs on
have on one's hands
have one's eye out for
put dibs on
to have and to hold

Practicality/ Pragmatism

game is not worth the candle
get down to brass tacks
get down to cases
get down to the nitty-gritty

Persuasion/ Persuasiveness

bring around
buy off
come to bear
eat out of one's hand
hold water
snow job
talk a good line
talk into
talk out of
talking point

Preparedness/ Preparation

armed to the teeth
beat the gun
gird one's loins
know what one is getting
    oneself into
psych oneself up
ready, willing, and able
take a deep breath

take a long breath
take aim
take arms
take up arms

fork over
make with
shell out

Presence

darken one's door
in absentia
in at the kill
in for the kill
in person
in the flesh
on board
present and accounted for
put in an appearance
set foot in
set foot on

Prevention

bar the door

Production

cough up
deliver the goods

Progress

cover ground
from strength to strength
get a jump on
get ahead
get around
get at
get on with it
get someplace
get somewhere
get to first base
growing pains
home in on
in due course
in due season
in due time
in good season
in good time
in the clear
make a dent in
make head
make one's way
make one's way in the world
make way
move along
on the march
on the mend
on the move
on the way
onward and upward
onwards and upwards

out from under
out of the hole
out of the woods
over the hump
pick one's way
piece by piece
push on
rags-to-riches
step by step
up-and-coming

Promotion

make a pitch
play up
put in a good word for
talk it up
talk up

Protective Action

hit the deck
hit the dirt
hole in
hole up

Protective Distance

at arm's length
stand off

Protest

kick up
kick up a fuss
kick up a row
kick up dust
make noises
scream bloody murder

Providentiality

lay away
lay by
lay in
put aside
salt away
save for a rainy day
save up
scrimp and save
stock up
tighten one's belt
waste not, want not

Prudence

a little knowledge is a
    dangerous thing
feather one's nest
just in case
keep a civil tongue in one's
    head
keep a low profile
keep at a distance
keep at arm's length
keep one's distance
keep one's nose clean
keep one's powder dry
let sleeping dogs lie
let well enough alone
look before one leaps
mum's the word
play it close to the vest
play it safe
quit while one is ahead
stick to one's knitting
take care
tend to one's knitting

Pursuit

give chase
go after
hunt down
hunt up
on one's heels
on the track of
on the trail of

run after
run to earth
run to ground
tag after
take out after
track down

Question

call into question
in question
see the color of one's money

Readiness/ Preparedness

at one's beck and call
at one's service
at the drop of a hat
at the ready
fit for duty
on call
on deck
on one's mettle
on tap
on the alert
raring to go
square away
warm up

Reality

birds and bees
face facts
facts are facts
facts of life
moment of truth
slice-of-life
walk into with one's eyes wide
    open

Rebellion

hit the bricks
kick against the pricks
kick over the traces

Recovery

get one's act together
get one's head on straight
get over
lick one's wounds
snap back
snap out of it

Regression

roll back
set back
setback

Rejection

close one's eyes to
close the door
cold shoulder
get the air
get the brush-off
get the bum's rush
get the gate
give the go-by
go hang
go pound nails
go pound salt
go pound sand
go to blazes
go to grass
go to hell
good riddance
good riddance to bad rubbish
have no use for
have none of
hell you say
kick out
kiss off
kiss-off
like hell
muscle out

no deal
no dice
no go
no sale
no way
none of one's beeswax
none of one's business
not give the time of day
nothing doing
out in the cold
put it where the sun don't
  shine
shove it
throw out
throw over
throw to the wolves
toss out
turn a cold shoulder to
turn down
turn one's back on
turn out
turn thumbs down
turn up one's nose
wash one's hands of
wipe one's hands of

Reprimand

bawl out
rake over the coals
rap on the knuckles
slap on the wrist
take to task
talk like a Dutch uncle
talking-to
tell off
tell what to do with
tell where to get off
tell where to head in
tongue-lashing

Resourcefulness

card up one's sleeve
have it in one
in reserve
ways and means

Removal

boot out
kick out
kill off
stamp out

Restraint

get off one's back
hold back
hold down
hold everything
hold off

hold one's fire
hold one's temper
hold one's tongue
in check
keep back
keep down
keep it down
keep off one's back
keep on ice
keep on the back burner
keep one's hands off
keep one's mitts off
keep one's mouth shut
keep one's nose out of
keep one's temper
keep one's trap shut
lay off
leave alone
leave it be
leave it lie
leave well enough alone
let alone
let be
let it lie
let up on
look but don't touch
mind one's beeswax
mind one's business
off one's back
pipe down
pull a punch
pull in
rein in
tie down
tie up
trim one's sails
zip one's lip

Retreat

back down
back off
back out
beat a retreat
bow out
cop out
draw in one's horns
fall back
haul down one's colors
on the run
pull in one's ears
pull in one's neck

Retribution

chickens come home to roost
come home to roost
devil to pay
dose of one's own medicine
eye for an eye and a tooth for a
    tooth
fix one's little red wagon
fix one's wagon
get one's lumps
get what's coming
have coming
have it coming
have one's hide
pay off
pay the fiddler
pay the piper

pay through the nose
payoff
price on one's head
serve one right
taste of one's own medicine

Revelation

bare one's breast
bare one's soul
blow one's cover
bring to light
bring up
come out
come out of the closet
get off one's chest
give away
give oneself away
go public
let on
let the cat out of the bag
make public
out in the open
put one into the picture
put wise
show one's colors
show one's hand
show one's true colors
spill the beans
tip one's hand
tip one's mitt
trip up

Revenge

get even
give a taste of one's own
    medicine
have it in for
have one's own back
settle a score
settle an old score
settle the score
wipe out an old score

Revival

come back
come back to earth
come back down to earth
comeback

Risk

ask for trouble
buy a pig in a poke
cast bread upon the waters
fly blind
fly by the seat of one's pants
go for broke
go for the brass ring
go out on a limb

go the vole
high roller
high-wire act
in the balance
long shot
look for trouble
odds-on
play it close
play with fire
press one's luck
push one's luck
ride for a fall
run a risk
skate on thin ice
stick one's chin out
stick one's neck out
take a chance
take one's chances
take one's life in one's hands
take the plunge
there's many a slip
there's many a slip 'twixt the
  cup and the lip
throw caution to the winds
tightrope act

poke and pry
poke around
pound the pavement
scare up
scrape up
scrounge around
search high and low
search out
search with a fine-tooth comb
smell out
sniff out

Second-guessing

back-seat driver
Monday-morning
  quarterback

Secrecy

behind closed doors
behind the scenes
between the lines
between you, me, and the
  lamppost
cat-and-mouse
cloak-and-dagger
closed-door
entre nous
hush up

Search

in quest of
in search of
in the market for
leave no stone unturned
look for
nose around
poke about

hush-hush
in secret
keep from
keep the lid on
keep to oneself
keep under one's hat
lie low
off-the-record
on the q.t.
on the quiet
on the sly
paper over
skeleton in the closet
sneak by
stow away
under cover
under one's breath
under one's hat
under the counter
under the nose of
under the table
under wraps
up one's sleeve
whitewash

Setback

body blow
kick in the pants
kick in the teeth
knock back on one's heels
knock for a loop

Showing Off

ham it up
look, Ma, no hands
loudmouth
put through one's paces
show off
show-off
take the floor

Silence

hold one's tongue
save one's breath
shut one's bazoo
shut one's face
shut one's mouth
shut one's trap
shut one's yap
shut up

Seizure

get one's hands on
lay hold of
lay one's hands on
seize upon

Start

from the ground up
from the top
from the word go
get cracking
get going
get off one's duff
get off one's tail
get off the ground
get on the ball
get on the stick
get the ball rolling
get the show on the road
kick off
lead off
lead the way
let 'er rip
let it rip
start off
start off with a bang
start out
start the ball rolling
start up
strike up
touch off
wade in

Starting Over

back to square one
back to the drawing board
back to the old drawing board

Strong Action

bring out the big guns
bring out the heavy artillery
come out swinging
give it all one's got
give it both barrels
jump in with both feet
take charge
take over
wade in

Study

brush up
hit the books

Success

ace in the hole
ahead of the game
all in one piece
A-OK
beat to the draw
beat to the punch
big box office
box office
brass ring
bring down the house
bring off

catch fire
climb the ladder
climb the ladder of success
come through
come up smelling like roses
come up to expectations
come up to snuff
find pay dirt
get there
go over big
go places
have it knocked
have it made
have it made in the shade
hit an all-time high
hit pay dirt
hit the jackpot
in like Flynn
in the bag
land-office business
make a go of
make a hit
make out
make the grade
measure up
nothing succeeds like success
on top
over the top
pan out
pull off
rags-to-riches
ride high
rise in the world
sell like hotcakes
set the world on fire
smash hit
strike it rich
strike pay dirt
take a bow

take off
ten-strike
with flying colors

Suddenness

at a blow
at a stroke
at one fell swoop
before one can say Jack
   Robinson
before one knows it
bob up
bolt from the blue
hit-and-run
in a flash
in one fell swoop
out of thin air
take it into one's head

Summoning

knock up
order up
ring in
ring up
send for

Support

go to bat for
in back of
in behalf of
in one's behalf
shore up
stand behind
stand by

Surprise

catch in the act
catch with one's pants down
creep up on
hang on to one's hat
hold on to one's hat
miracle of miracles
out of the mouths of babes
sneak up on
take by surprise
throw a curve
throw for a loop
throw for a loss
wonder of wonders

Surrender

give oneself up
run up the white flag
say uncle

throw in the sponge
throw in the towel
throw up one's hands
throw up the sponge
toss in the towel

Survival

bread and butter
break even
can hack it
get over
get through
get through in one piece
God tempers the wind to the
  shorn lamb
keep body and soul together
keep one's feet
keep one's head above water
keep the wolf from the door
land on both feet
land on one's feet
live from hand to mouth
make do
make ends meet
pull through
save one's neck
save one's skin
sink or swim
tread water

Suspense

cross one's fingers
hang in the balance
hang over one's head
hold one's breath
keep one's fingers crossed
leave hanging
leave hanging in the air
live on borrowed time
lull before the storm
on the edge of one's chair
on the edge of one's seat
on the point of
sweat blood
sweat bullets
unknown quantity

third degree
trial and error
trial balloon
try on for size
try out

Travel

hit the road
hit the sawdust trail
on the road
ride shank's mare
ride shank's pony

Test

litmus test
on trial
pass for
pass inspection
pass muster
proof of the pudding is in the
    eating
put to the sword
put to the test
run-through
seeing is believing
separate the men from the
    boys
sound out

Uproar

all hell breaks loose
big stink
hue and cry
make the feathers fly
make the fur fly
raise the dead
slam-bang
three-ring circus
whoop-de-do
whooping and hollering

Vagrancy

bum around

Victory

carry the palm
get the last laugh
go over big
go over in a big way
have the last laugh
he who laughs last laughs best
run away with
save the day
sweep the board
sweep the table
walk away from
walk away with
walk off with
walkover
win out
winning streak

Waiting

bide one's time
cool one's heels
lay for
lay over
lie by
on the bench
on the string
sit it out
sit out
stand in the wings
stick around
warm the bench

Warning

gangway
heads up
on notice
watch it
watch out

Visiting

drop in on
look in on
stop by
stop in
stop off
stop over

Wasting Time

dawdle
fiddle around

Withdrawal

beat a retreat
bow out
build a wall around oneself
cold turkey
drop out
get away
in a shell
opt out
out of circulation
out of the limelight
out of the picture
out of the running
out of the swim
pull away
pull out

step down
take back
tune out
turn off
turn one's back

Yielding

give an inch
give ground
give in
give over
give way
part with

Behavior

Frivolousness

fiddle around
fool around
for the hell of it
fun and games
happy-go-lucky
hell around
light-headed
light-minded
lose one's head
mess around
monkey around
monkey business
much ado about nothing
pull one's leg
rattlebrained
simple-minded
slaphappy
vanity fair

Ill Manners

brought up in a barn
ill-bred
ill-mannered
wash one's dirty linen in
    public

Imprudence

a fool and his money are soon
    parted
borrow trouble
burn a hole in one's pocket
fools rush in
fools rush in where angels fear
    to tread
go off the deep end
jump off the deep end

kill the goose that laid the golden egg
let the cat out of the bag
lock the barn door after the horse is stolen
put all one's eggs in one basket
slip of the lip
slip of the tongue
throw caution to the winds
throw discretion to the winds

leave to one's own devices
let go of one's mother's apron strings
lone wolf
make it on one's own
of one's own accord
of one's own free will
off one's own bat
on one's own
on one's own account
on one's own hook
on one's own time
one's own man
paddle one's own canoe
pay one's own way
shift for oneself
stand on one's own feet
stand on one's own two feet
strong-minded
under one's own steam

Impudence

answer back
give one lip
smart aleck
smart-alecky
smarty-pants
talk back

Independence

every man for himself
go Dutch
go it alone
hoe one's own row
help oneself
in one's own right
jump the traces
law unto oneself

Indiscretion

big mouth
big-mouthed
kiss and tell
let the cat out of the bag
loudmouth
loud-mouthed
mouth off
shoot off one's face
shoot off one's mouth
spill the beans
tell tales out of school
wash one's dirty linen in public

Inhibition

cramp one's style
crepehanger

Laziness

goof off
lazybones

Irresponsibility

asleep at the switch
asleep on the job
buck passer
buck-passing
devil-may-care
for the hell of it
forget oneself
go hog-wild
go off half-cocked
go wild
harum-scarum
let George do it
lie down on the job
old army game
penny-wise and pound-foolish
play fast and loose
sow one's wild oats
take the law into one's own
   hands
trigger-happy

Leader

big cheese
big enchilada
big frog in a little pond
big frog in a small pond
big gun
big shot
big wheel
bigwig
head honcho
number one
numero uno

Menace

bark is worse than one's bite

Mischief

fool around
get gay
hell around
high jinks
horse around

Obedience

brownie points
come to heel
earn brownie points
in line
jump through a hoop
knuckle under
law-abiding
take orders
toe the line
toe the mark
walk chalk
walk the chalk line
walk the chalk mark

Observation

get a load of
give a look
give the once-over
have one eye on

keep a watchful eye
keep a weather eye open
keep an eye on
lay eyes on
look on
look over
meet one's eye
on sight
on the lookout
on the watch
open-eyed
out of the corner of one's eye
set eyes on
take a gander at
take note of
take notice of
tell apart

Partisanship

cast in one's lot with
cast one's lot with
keep the faith
side against
side by side
side with
stick up for
take sides
throw in one's lot with
true-hearted

Passivity

lying down
mama's boy
meek as a lamb
namby-pamby
nervous Nellie
shrinking violet
sit back
sit by
sit like a bump on a log
take lying down

Pretense

barracks lawyer
come off it
give oneself airs
make believe
play at
play dead
play dumb
play possum
play the part
sail under false colors

Regularity

as a rule
go to bed with the chickens
like clockwork
on the hour
set one's watch by

Relaxation

at ease
at one's ease
at home
at rest
breathe easily
breathe easy
breathe freely
calm down
cool down
cool off
forget oneself
get a load off one's feet
go easy
goof off
laid-back
loose as a goose
park one's carcass
sit back
slow down
slow up
take a load off one's feet
take five
take it easy
take one's time
take things easy
time out

Restlessness

ants in one's pants
climb the walls
not sleep a wink
toss and turn
walk the floor

Self-defeat

cut off one's nose to spite
  one's face
cut one's own throat
put one's head in a noose

Self-indulgence

for the fun of it
for the hell of it
just for kicks

Self-injury

blow one's brains out
hoist by one's own petard
hoist with one's own petard
sign one's own death warrant

Selfishness

dog in the manger
every man for himself
play both sides against the
  middle
play off both ends against the
  middle
save one's own neck
save one's own skin

Self-satisfaction

have money in the bank
laugh in one's beard
laugh in one's sleeve
laugh up one's sleeve
look as if butter wouldn't melt
  in one's mouth
look like the cat that ate the
  canary
look like the cat that swallowed
  the canary
pat oneself on the back

Servility

bow down to
curry favor
lick one's boots

Suitability

act one's age
be one's age
fit like a glove
fit the bill
fit to a T
made for each other

Submission

cry uncle
lie down and play dead
take lying down
take one's medicine

Threat

breathe down one's neck
hang over one's head
paper tiger
raise a finger
raise a hand
read the riot act
saber-rattling
sword-rattling
under pain of

Subservience

bow and scrape
curry favor
dogsbody
on bended knee
on one's knees
play second fiddle
running dog
throw oneself at one's feet
wait on
wait on hand and foot

Timeserving

clock watcher
mark time
timeserver

Tolerance

each to his own
different strokes for different
  folks
live and let live
lump it
make allowance
put up with
take a joke
turn the other cheek
wink at

Unfitting Behavior

act the fool
like a bull in a china shop
make a fool of oneself
make an ass of oneself
use the wrong fork
zigged when one should have
  zagged

Uninhibitedness

feel free
feel one's oats
flat out
free and easy
free as a bird

free as the breeze
lay it on
lay it on me
let it all hang out
let loose
let off steam
let one's hair down
let oneself go
make free with
out loud

Unsuitable Behavior

act up
air one's dirty line in public
bad actor
bull in a china shop
cut the comedy
play hooky
raise Cain
raise heck
raise hell

Vacillation

change horses in midstream
change horses in the middle
  of the stream
change one's tune
come and go

coming and going
every now and again
every now and then
every so often
feast or famine
from pillar to post
from time to time
off-again, on-again
off-and-on
on-again, off-again
on-and-off
pillar to post
shilly-shally
sing a different tune
sing a new tune
take turns
to and fro
whistle a different tune
whistle a new tune

Vanity

big head
blow one's own horn
cock of the walk
on an ego trip
plume oneself
stuck on oneself
swell-headed
swelled head
think one is God's gift
toot one's own horn
turn one's head

Communication

Abuse

badmouth
call names
kick around
name-calling
ride roughshod over
shirt on
skin alive

Accommodation

bend over backward
bend over backwards
climb on the bandwagon
come around
come down off one's high
    horse
come over
come round
come to terms
common ground
get off one's high horse
if you can't beat them, join
    them
lean over backward
lean over backwards
lend oneself to
make a virtue of necessity
make room
make the best of it
make way
meet halfway
middle ground
move over

Accusation

cast the first stone
lay at one's door
pin on

pin the blame on
pin the rap on
point the finger
pot calling the kettle black
put the finger on

come right out
in no uncertain terms
make no bones about

Boasting

blow off
blow one's own horn

Achievement

get to first base
have a good thing going
make the grade
make one's mark
reach first base

Commentary

say a mouthful
say in so many words
say one's piece

Assistance

help out
lend a hand
on one's coattails
open doors
ride on one's coattails

Communication

by word of mouth
drop a line
express oneself
get through to
get to
open up
pass it on
put across
spread the word

Bluntness

black-and-white
call a spade a spade

Complaint

badmouth
find fault
pet peeve
raise a fuss
rant and rave
sound off

Criticism

badmouth
bawl out
bone to pick
call a spade a spade
call on the carpet
call to account
cast the first stone
chew out
come down hard on
cut to pieces
cut to ribbons
dress down
find fault
haul over the coals
jump all over
jump on one's case
lace into
lay into
lay out
lay out in lavender
let have it
let have it with both barrels
lower the boom
make it hot for
people who live in glass
    houses shouldn't throw
    stones
pick a hole in
pick apart
pick at
pick to pieces
piece of one's mind
pull down
put down
put-down
rake over the coals
ream out
take apart
tear down
tee off on
tell a thing or two

Defiance

call one's bluff
how do you like them apples
make something of it
make something out of it
says who
says you
sez you
show a thing or two
so's your old man
spit in one's eye
stick it

Detail

blow by blow
ins and outs
dot the i's
play-by-play
spell it out
spell out
whys and wherefores

Encouragement

bring out
bring out of one's shell
carrot and stick
lift one's spirits
pat on the back
pep talk
push for
shot in the arm
take heart
way to go
with one all the way

Farewell

catch you later
see off
see out
see you

see you around
see you in church
see you later
see you later, alligator
swan song

Glibness

butter wouldn't melt in one's
    mouth
fast talker
silver-tongued
smooth-tongued

Gossip

carry tales
cause tongues to wag
dish the dirt
ears burn
fan the breeze
make tongues wag
tell tales
tell tales out of school
whispering campaign

Inarticulateness

cat has one's tongue
lose one's tongue
stick in one's throat

Inscrutability

closed book

Isolation

burn one's bridges
burn one's bridges behind one
lone wolf
out in the cold
out of circulation
out of it
shut off

Incomprehension

blind leading the blind
it's all Dutch to me
it's all Greek to me
look blank
not know which way is up
over one's head
talk Dutch
talk Greek

Levity

crack a joke
crack a smile
in stitches
kid around
kid the pants off of
laugh it up
split one's sides
tongue-in-cheek

Information

clue in
get the word
get wind of
tip off
tip-off

Loudness

at the top of one's lungs
at the top of one's voice
give voice
loud and clear
to the rafters

Meeting

brainstorming
go into a huddle
put heads together

Nonsense

banana oil
stuff and nonsense

Relevance

come to the point
come to think of it
have to do with
in light of

in line with
in the light of
to the point

Rhetorical Questions and Statements

how about that
how do you like them apples
says who
says you
sez you
what about that
what of it
what's cooking
what's doing
what's happening
what's the big idea
what's up

Talk

bat the breeze
chew the fat
chew the rag
gift of gab
gift of the gab
hold forth
line of gab
line of talk

rattle off
rattle on
reel off
run off at the mouth
run on
shoot the breeze
shoot the bull

spit it out
talk a blue streak
talk one's ear off
talk oneself blue in the face
talk until one is blue in the face
think aloud
think out loud

Duty

Accountability

lay at one's door
lay at one's doorstep

Burden

hang heavy
hang heavy on one's hands
have a monkey on one's back
house of Atreus
on one's shoulders

Avoidance

buck-passing
give a wide berth
palm off
pass the buck
shy away
shy off
steer clear

Commitment

fat is in the fire
give one's heart
go the whole hog
have too many irons in the fire
hold to
hold to account
in deep
in for a dime, in for a dollar
labor of love
on the line

Custom

as usual
business as usual
by the numbers
make a habit of
make a practice of
make the rounds
matter of course
of course
of old
out of habit
port of call

Discipline

come down hard on
crack down
crack the whip
draw the line
lower the boom

Discretion

all in the family
button one's lips
in private
keep mum
keep one's own counsel
keep one's powder dry
mum's the word

Dependability

as good as one's promise
as good as one's word

Devotion

give oneself over to
give oneself up to
throw oneself into

Duty

climb on the bandwagon
cling to one's mother's apron
    strings
line of duty

Indecisiveness

back and forth
fall between two stools
fence-sitting
namby-pamby
off-and-on
on the fence
on-and-off
sit on the fence
straddle the fence
wishy-washy

Penalty

catch it
catch it in the neck
hell to pay
pay the piper
price on one's head
price to pay

Promptness

behind time
better late than never
bright and early
on the dot

Involvement

have irons in the fire
have too many irons in the fire
in deep
in deep water
in up to the chin
in up to the eyeballs
iron in the fire
knee-deep
neck-deep
soil one's hands
tie up
wrapped up in

Regimen

by the numbers
spit and polish
stand on ceremony

Respect

in awe of
in honor of

in memory of
red-carpet treatment
roll out the red carpet
stand in awe of
take off one's hat to
think a great deal of
think a lot of
think the world of
time-honored

Responsibility

ball in one's court
carry the ball
carry the weight of the world
carry the weight of the world
   on one's shoulders
devil to pay
duty bound
have on one's hands

hold one's end up
hold the bag
hold the sack
hold to
hold to account
hold up one's end
in one's court
in the line of duty
keep one's end up
keep up one's end
lay at one's door
lay on one
let off the hook
off one's hands
off the hook
on one's head
on one's shoulders
order of business
out of one's hands
shoulder the burden
take care of
take it upon oneself
take upon oneself
up to one

Emotion

Affection

be crazy about
be crazy for
be mad about
be mad for
be nuts about
be nuts for
be nuts over
be stuck on
be sweet on
be wild about
calf love
crazy in love
fall for
fall head over heels
hold hands with
labor of love
love to death
love to pieces
nutty about
nutty over
sweet on

Affinity

cup of tea
cut out to be
dish of tea
down one's alley
down one's street
go in for
have a way with
like a duck takes to water
natural-born
nose for
run in the blood
run in the family

Aggravate

add insult to injury
pour salt in the wound

Aimlessness

around Robin Hood's barn
go around in circles
go in circles
in a circle
knock about
knock around
rattle around

Amorousness

fling woo
go a-sparking
have a crush on
have eyes for
have eyes only for
hold hands
in love
lose one's heart
love up
make a play for
make eyes at
make goo-goo eyes
make love
make time with
on the make
pitch woo
play footsie
puppy love

Anger

blow a fuse
blow a gasket
blow one's cool
blow one's stack
blow one's top
blow up
boiling point
burn up
burst a blood vessel
fit to be tied
get one's back up
get one's dander up
get one's Irish up
high dudgeon
hit the ceiling
hit the roof
loaded for bear
look daggers
lose one's cool
lose one's temper
mad as a hornet
mad as a wet hen
mad as hops
make one's blood boil
on the warpath
pop one's cork
purple with rage
see red
short fuse
slow burn
steamed up
ticked off

Animosity

bad blood
break with
death on
end on a sour note
get off on the wrong foot
hate one's guts
no love lost
on the outs

Anxiety

at loose ends
at one's wit's end
at sixes and sevens
beside oneself
butterflies in one's stomach
cold feet
jump out of one's skin
nerve-racking
nervous in the service
nervous Nellie
off one's head
on edge
on pins and needles
on the hot seat
screaming meemies

Appreciation

feast one's eyes on

Appropriateness

cup of tea
cut out to be
dish of tea
down one's alley
down one's street
fit the bill
fit to a T
hand-and-glove
hand-in-glove
if the shoe fits, wear it
in character
in keeping
just what the doctor ordered
run true to form

Approval

clean bill of health
earn brownie points
get on the good side of
give the devil his due
give the go-ahead
give the green light

green light
pat on the back
pat oneself on the back

Bias

all for
in favor of

Astonishment

are you kidding
believe one's ears
bug-eyed
cockeyed wonder
do a double take
knock for a loop
knock one out
knock one over
knock one over with a feather
knock one's hat off
knock one's socks off
make one's eyes bug out
make one's eyes pop out
open-mouthed
pull up short
raise eyebrows
set back on one's heels
small wonder
take aback

Boredom

bore to death
bore to tears
fed up with
had it up to here with
sick and tired
sick to death

Cajolery

butter up
make nice-nice
make nice to
soft soap
soft-soap
sweet talk
sweet-talk

Awkwardness

fish out of water
stand with one's face hanging
    out

Calmness

bat an eye
bat an eyelash
cool as a cucumber
cool as ice
cool down
cool off
drop a stitch
easygoing
have it all together
low-key
matter-of-fact
mellow out
nice and quiet
not to worry
play it cool
presence of mind
pull oneself together
quiet as a church
quiet as a mouse
settle down
simmer down

Cheerfulness

light-hearted
light up

Comfort

at ease
at home
bed of roses
cold comfort
comfortable as an old shoe
easy street
easy to take
in clover

Compassion

find it in one's heart
have a heart
have one's heart in the right
    place
heart goes out to
heart of gold
large-hearted
let down easy
let off easy
open-hearted
open one's heart
take pity on
tender-hearted
warm-hearted
whole-hearted

Conceit

big head
full of oneself
go to one's head
know-it-all
stuck-up

Cowardice

afraid of one's own shadow
beat a retreat
chicken-livered
chicken-out
lily-livered
show the white feather
yellow-bellied

Concern

give a damn
give a darn
give a hoot
give a tinker's damn
go out of one's way
handle with kid gloves
in behalf of
look after
on behalf of
take to heart

Depression

blue Monday
burn out
crepehanger
down in the dumps
down-in-the-mouth
have the blues
in the dumps
in the pits
morning after

Contentment

happy as a clam
happy as a clam at high tide
happy as a lark
in all one's glory
in hog heaven
in one's glory

Despair

in the pits
no use
slough of despond

Disappointed Expectations

blow up in one's face
bottom drop out
bottom fall out
break one's heart
burn out
die on the vine
end on a sour note
fall short
fall through
let down
no show
slap in the face

go against the grain
ill at ease
in a bad way
like a fish out of water
on the hot seat
out of one's element

Discouragement

dash cold water on
lose heart

Disapproval

make a face
silent treatment
take a dim view of

Disfavor/Disrepute

behind the eight ball
fall from grace
get off on the wrong foot with
in bad
in bad odor
in one's bad graces
in the doghouse
in wrong
on one's bad side
on the bad side of
put one in Dutch with
sour on
start off on the wrong foot with
think little of
wouldn't give the time of day
     to

Discomfort

close to home
close to the bone
feel a draft

Disgust

fed to the gills
fed to the teeth
fed up
gross one out
had it up to here
make one sick
turn one off
turn one's stomach
turnoff

Embarrassment

blow one's cool
go pink
like to die
like to have died
make one's ears burn
make one's ears turn pink
put on the spot
red as a beet
red in the face
sore point
sore spot
turn color

Emotion

not a dry eye in the house
pin one's heart to one's sleeve

pour out one's heart
pull out all the stops
rant and rave
tug at one's heartstrings
turn on the waterworks
wear one's heart on one's
    sleeve

Emotional Stress

all shook up
at loose ends
at one's wit's end
at sixes and sevens
basket case
blow one's cool
come apart
come apart at the seams
crack up
drive up the wall
end of one's rope
end of one's tether
fall apart
flip one's lid
flip one's wig
frazzled
freak out
go to pieces
have a lump in one's throat
have fits
hung up
jimjams
jitters
lose one's grip
on the rack
shook up

storm and stress
stress and strain
Sturm und Drang
tie in knots
tie oneself in knots
uptight
war of nerves
wild-eyed

Empathy/Sympathy

common touch
feel for
good vibes
good vibrations
in one's boots
in one's shoes
in someone else's shoes
on one's wavelength
play upon
put oneself in another's place
put oneself in another's shoes

be wild about
big on
crazy over
eager beaver
early bird catches the worm
fall all over
fall head over heels
go all the way
go to town
go wild
gung ho
hot for
hot to go
hot to trot
mad about
mad for
make much of
nuts over
nutty about
nutty over
pep talk
switched-on
way to go
wild about
with bells on
with knobs on

Enthusiasm

be crazy about
be crazy for
be mad about
be mad for
be nuts about
be nuts for

Envy

grass is always greener on the
    other side of the fence
grass is always greener on the
    other side of the hill
green with envy

Euphoria

feel like a million
feel like a million dollars
have one's head in the clouds
heaven on earth
on cloud nine
on top of the world
paradise on earth
pleased as punch
ride high
sit on top of the world
stars in one's eyes

Exasperation

for crying out loud
get in one's hair
get on one's nerves
get one's back up
get one's goat
get under one's skin
give fits
give one gray hair
give one a hard time
give one a pain
go against the grain
have had it
nerve-racking
put out
set one's teeth on edge
sick to death of
tear one's hair

Excitability

hot-blooded
keyed up
worked up

Excitement

beside oneself
blow one's cool
blow one's mind
burst a blood vessel
climb the walls
fast and furious
flip one's lid
flip one's wig
fly high
get off on
go ape
go into orbit
have a fit
have fits
have kittens
have one's heart miss a beat
have one's heart skip a beat
have one's heart stand still
high as a kite
hopped up
in a spin
in a tailspin
in orbit
jump around
on pins and needles

spine-chilling
spine-tingling
turn one on
turn-on
whoop it up
whoop-de-do
wing-ding
worked up

have one's heart skip a beat
have one's heart stand still
scare out of one's wits
scare the daylights out of
scare to death
scared stiff
scaredy-cat
shake in one's boots
shake in one's shoes
shake like a leaf
stage fright
weak-hearted
white with fear

Expectation

live up to
pin one's hopes on

Hopefulness

ghost of a chance
great hopes from little acorns
    grow
have a prayer
have one's heart set on
hope against hope
if only
in hopes
keep one's fingers crossed
knock on wood
ray of hope
ray of sunshine
see the light at the end of the
    tunnel
stand a chance
wishful thinking
wishing won't make it so

Exuberance

joie de vivre
jump for joy
kick up one's heels

Fear

fear and trembling
have one's heart in one's
    mouth
have one's heart miss a beat

Horror

blood runs cold
blood turns to ice
freeze one's blood
freeze the blood in one's veins
give the creeps
give the willies
hair stand on end
jump out of one's skin
make one's blood run cold
make one's hair stand on end
spine-chilling
spine-tingling

Imperturbability

bat an eye
bat an eyelash
cut no ice

Impetuosity

headstrong
hotheaded

Hostility

bad blood
chip on one's shoulder
come to blows
cross swords
death on
on the warpath
push comes to shove

Impatience

ants in one's pants
champ at the bit
hold no brief for

Indifference

devil-may-care
don't give a damn
don't give a hoot
go chase oneself
go fly a kite
go jump in the lake
go through the motions
like water off a duck's back
no skin off one's nose
rest on one's laurels
rest on one's oars
slack off
take it or leave it

Intuition

feel in one's bones
know in one's bones
sixth sense

Mood

happy as a clam
happy as a clam at high tide
happy as a lark

Irritability

get up on the wrong side of the
    bed
get up out of the wrong side of
    bed
have one's nose in a sling
off-color
on edge
out of sorts
put one's nose out of joint
quick-tempered

Offense

cut to the quick
gross out
hard feelings
hurt to the quick
slap in the face
take amiss

Optimism

chin up
every cloud has a silver lining
every dog has his day
hope against hope
it's an ill wind that blows no
    good
it's an ill wind that blows
    nobody good
keep one's chin up
look at the world through
    rose-colored glasses
look on the bright side
thumbs up

Jealousy

green with envy
green-eyed monster
sour grapes

Out of Control

around the bend
in over one's head
out of one's hands
round the bend
run riot
run wild
tailspin

Reaction

get a rise out of

Reassurance

cold comfort

Overreaction

beside oneself
burst a blood vessel
chew the scenery
go off half-cocked
go off the deep end
go overboard
have a fit
jump the gun
jump to conclusions

Regret

heartsick
if only
kick oneself
laugh on the other side of
    one's mouth
laugh on the wrong side of
    one's mouth
laugh out of the other side of
    one's face
laugh out of the other side of
    one's mouth
more's the pity
rue the day

Pride

hold one's head up
look one in the eye

Release

break up
cut loose
let fly
let go
let loose
let off
let out
set free
set loose

Repression

bottle up
sit on
slap down
swallow one's pride
swallow one's words

Resentment

hard feelings
have a chip on one's shoulder
have an ax to grind

Relief

blow off
blow off steam
breathe easily
breathe easy
breathe freely
draw a long breath
get off one's chest
get off one's conscience
get off one's mind
kick the habit
out of one's hair
out of one's hands
sight for sore eyes

Satisfaction

get off
get off on
hit the spot
music to one's ears
so far, so good
strike a happy medium
to one's heart content

Reluctance

far be it from me
hang back

Sadness

down in the dumps
heavy heart
heavy-hearted
in the dumps
in the pits
long face

Shock

curl your hair
drop a bomb
drop a bombshell
drop a brick
drop one's cookies
explode a bombshell
kick in the pants
kick in the teeth
knock for a loop

Sentimentality

cornball
cry in one's beer
misty-eyed
pin one's heart on one's
  sleeve
sob sister
sob story

Yearning

give one's eyeteeth
give one's right arm
have an itch

Shame

can't hold one's head up
hang one's head
hide one's face
hide one's head
hit an all-time low
hit bottom
tail between one's legs

Mental World

Absurdity

cockeyed
from the sublime to the
  ridiculous

Analysis

get to the bottom of
get to the heart of
get to the point
hash out
have one pegged
psych out
size up
take apart

Anonymity

Jane Doe
Joe Doaks
John Doe
John Q. Public
man in the street
man jack
Richard Roe
so-and-so

Approximation

after a fashion
in the ball park
just about
more or less
next door to
nowhere near

on the order of
or so
sort of

Clearheadedness

clear as a bell
cold sober

Concentration

brown study
buckle down
burn the midnight oil
crack a book
cudgel one's brains
dope out
fall into a brown study
have one's nose in a book
have one's nose to the
    grindstone
knuckle down
learn by heart
lose oneself in
mind over matter
peg away
put on one's thinking cap
put one's mind to
single-minded
turn to

Confusion

at a loss
at loose ends
at sea
at sixes and sevens
blind alley
blind leading the blind
cart before the horse
cockeyed
cross wires
fall all over oneself
get one's signals crossed
have the cart before the horse
helter-skelter
hugger-mugger
in a fog
in a haze
in circles
in orbit
it's all Dutch to me
it's all Greek to me
know if one is coming or going
know whether one is coming
    or going
know which way is up
know which way to turn
let the left hand not know
    what the right hand is doing
mare's nest
mix-up
mixed up
nobody home
not know which way to jump
not know which way to turn
out of it
rattlebrained
screwed up
throw off
throw off the scent

Consciousness

hear bells
in the know
keep in mind
know from nothing
open one's eyes
open up one's eyes
put in mind
see beyond one's nose
see beyond the end of one's
   nose
soak in

Consequence

chickens come home to roost
in the wake of
in turn
stew in one's own juice

Consideration

in view
kick around
knock around
look upon
mull over
reckon with
sleep on it

take account of
take into account
take into consideration
under the circumstances
with an eye to

Contempt

heap scorn upon
hold one's nose
look down one's nose
look down upon
snap one's fingers at
take in vain
take one's name in vain
talk down to
thumb one's nose at
use one as a doormat
walk all over
walk over
wipe one's boots on
won't give the time of day

Craziness

around the bend
bats in one's belfry
be off one's trolley
crack up
cracked

crazy as a bedbug
crazy as a coot
crazy as a loon
crazy in the head
go bananas
go bonkers
go crackers
go crazy
go cuckoo
go haywire
go into a tailspin
go over the edge
have a hole in one's head
have a screw loose
have all one's buttons
have all one's marbles
have rocks in one's head
lose one's head
mad as a hatter
mad as a March hare
need to have one's head
  examined
not have all one's oars in the
  water
not playing with a full deck
nuttier than a fruitcake
nutty as a fruitcake
off one's chump
off one's head
off one's nut
off one's rocker
off one's trolley
off the wall
out of one's gourd
out of one's head
out of one's mind
out of one's senses
out of one's tree
slip a cog

slip a gear
touched in the head
wacko
wig out
without rhyme or reason

Denial

close one's eyes to
in a pig's eye
no thanks to
no way
not a bit of it
not at all
perish the thought
shut one's eyes to
turn a blind eye
turn a deaf ear

Disgrace

behind the eight ball
beyond the pale
can't show one's face in public
one's name is mud
under a cloud

Easement

balm in Gilead
balm of Gilead
bridge over troubled waters
lift one's spirits
lighten one's burden
lighten one's heart
path of least resistance
pave the way
pour oil on troubled waters
smooth away
smooth over
take off the edge
take the edge off of

eat crow
eat dirt
eat humble pie
eat one's words
feel like two cents
lose face
make a fool of
make a fool out of
make a monkey out of
one's name is mud
play for a chump
play for a fool
take down a notch
take down a peg
take down a peg or two
with one's tail between one's
    legs

Gullibility

buy a pig in a poke
lap up
swallow hook, line, and sinker
swallow whole
there's one born every minute

Humiliation

come down
come down in the world
comedown

Ideal

apple of one's eye
boy next door
fair-haired boy
girl next door
knight in shining armor
living end
made in heaven
made-to-measure
made-to-order
me plus ultra
peaches and cream
peachy keen
picture perfect
tailor-made
to a T
to a turn

Idealism

high-minded
hitch one's wagon to a star
never-never land
pie in the sky
promise one the moon
reach for the moon
reach for the sky
rose-colored glasses
see through rose-colored
    glasses
see with rose-colored glasses

Ignorance

be none the wiser
know beans
little does one know
little does one suspect
search me

Imagination

mind's eye
see in one's mind's eye
see things
think up
will-o'-the-wisp

Impracticality

airy-fairy
build castles in Spain
build castles in the air

Inattentiveness

asleep at the switch
asleep on the job
go in one ear and out the
    other
half an eye
head in the clouds
in another world
in one ear and out the other
wool-gather
woolgathering

Inspiration

bee in one's bonnet

Intelligence

bright as a button
bright as a new penny
good head on one's shoulders
have a mind like a steel trap
have something on the ball
horse sense
know a thing or two about
know enough to come in out
  of the rain
know one's business
know which side one's bread
  is buttered on
nobody's fool
quick-witted
ready-witted
sharp as a tack
smart as a whip

Invalidation

beat all hollow
beat hollow
knock into a cocked hat

Learning

bone up
cut one's eyeteeth on

Memory

in one's mind's eye
jog one's memory
look back
ring a bell

Mental Instability

fuzzy around the edges
light-headed
light-minded
lose one's head
lunatic fringe
not all there
not have all one's oars in the
  water
not playing with a full deck
punch-drunk
screwed up
spaced-out
tripped-out

Narrow-mindedness

can't see the forest for the
  trees
can't see the woods for the
  trees
Mickey Mouse

nitpicking
one-track
one-track mind
small-minded
spit and polish
split hairs

Perplexity

at a loss
at sea
closed book
fall into a brown study
hard nut to crack
horns of a dilemma
in the dark

Obsession

have on the brain
hung up on
into one's blood
on one's mind
queer for

Problem

hot potato
monkey on one's back

Patience

bide one's time
cat-and-mouse
cool one's heels
count to ten
fed up
give one enough rope and
    one will hang oneself
hold one's horses
keep one's shirt on
lie in wait
patience of Job
sit tight

Rationality

clear-headed
feast of reason
feet on the ground
keep one's wits about one
listen to reason
make sense
method in one's madness
rhyme or reason
right-minded
sound in mind
sound of mind
stand to reason

talk it out
talk over
talk sense
think out
think over
think through

like it or lump it
like it or not
live and let live
make one's bed and lie in it
so be it
that's the way the ball bounces
that's the way the cookie crumbles

Reconsideration

have second thoughts
on second thought
think twice

Skepticism

are you kidding
here goes nothing
I'm from Missouri; show me
put no stock in
take no stock in
take with a grain of salt
take with a pinch of salt
tell it to Sweeney
tell it to the Marines
that'll be the day

Resignation

all over but the shouting
back to the salt mines
be it so
can't fight City Hall
can't take it with one
come what may
easy come, easy go
easy does it
for better or for worse
for better or worse
forgive and forget
grin and bear it
let bygones be bygones
let it be
let the chips fall where they may

Stupidity

dumb bunny
dumb Dora
have a hole in one's head
have rocks in one's head
know enough to come in out of the rain
lame-brained

nobody home
nobody home upstairs
simple-minded
slow-witted
soft in the head
weak in the head
weak-minded
wooden-headed

Suggestion

bee in one's bonnet
bug in one's ear
flea in one's ear
give ideas
put forth
put forward
soft sell

Thought

in one's mind's eye
in the back of one's mind
in the clouds
pass through one's mind
put on one's thinking cap
put one's thinking cap on
put two and two together
rack one's brains
use one's bean
use one's head
use one's noggin
use one's noodle

Unrealistic Expectations

ask for the moon
build castles in Spain
build castles in the air
count one's chickens before
   they're hatched
pipe dream
shoot for the stars

Morality

Admission

cop a plea
let's face it
own up

Atonement

least said, soonest mended
mend one's fences

Bribery

cross one's palm
grease one's palm

grease the wheel
oil one's palm
one hand washes the other

Cheating

do out of
suck in
sucker into
sucker list

Coercion

breathe down one's neck
force one's hand
hard sell

look over one's shoulder
push to the wall
put the screws to
put the squeeze on
ram down one's throat
ride out of town
ride out of town on a rail
screw to the wall
shake down
smoke out
turn on the heat
twist one's arm
worm out of one

Contemptibility

lower than a snake
lower than a snake in the grass
snake in the grass

Debasement

dirty one's hands
hit rock bottom
touch bottom

Collusion

compare notes
gang up against
gang up on
in league with
put up to
thick as thieves

Deceit/Deception

do a Brodie
full of bull
full of hot air
full of it
get away with murder
get the runaround
hugger-mugger
lead on
line of bull
old army game
palm off
pass off
phony up
play fast and loose with
play head games

Concealment

cover one's tracks
cover up
cover up one's tracks

pull a Brodie
pull a fast one
pull one's leg
pull the wool over one's eyes
put one on
sail under false colors
sell a bill of goods
sell a pig in a poke
sell one a gold brick
sell one the Brooklyn Bridge
slip one over
slip something over on
snow job
under false colors
wolf in sheep's clothing

Destruction/ Destructiveness

bring down
bring down around one's ears
bump off
cut to pieces
cut to ribbons
go up in flames
go up in smoke
go up like smoke
mess up
nip in the bud
play havoc with
play hob with
play the devil with
put out of one's misery
put out of the way
put to death

Dishonesty

below the belt
buy off
cock-and-bull story
cut corners
do out of
have one's hands in the till
highway robbery
ill-gotten
ill-gotten gains
lie in one's teeth
lie through one's teeth
light-fingered
line one's pockets
line one's purse
mare's nest
monkey business
no-good
not playing with a full deck
pad the bill
rip off
rip-off
rob the till
sticky-fingered
sticky fingers
under the counter
under the table
up to no good
up to something
wheel and deal

Eccentricity

crackpot
odd man out
oddball
off the beam
off the beaten track
off the wall
off-center
off-key
offbeat
queer as a three-dollar bill

Entrapment

bring to bay
dead duck
dead to rights
have by the throat
have one's back against the
    wall
have one's back to the wall
in the middle
jig is up
trap like a rat
under arrest

Evasion/Evasiveness

beat the devil
beat the rap

beat the system
beg off
beg the question
bury one's head in the sand
get the run-around
give the slip
gloss over
go see a man about a dog
go see a man about a horse
have one's head in the sand
hide one's head in the sand
lead a merry chase
put one's head in the sand
run-around
slip past
smoke screen
throw off the scent
weasel out

Evidence

have something on
have the goods on

Exposure

blow one's cover
blow sky high
blow the lid off
blow the whistle on
give the lie to

show one's hand
show up

Fabrication

cook up
make up out of whole cloth
trump up

Fairness

give the benefit of the doubt
on the square
play fair
play fair and square
raw deal

Falsehood

cock-and-bull story
fish story
load of bull

Falseness

a crock
all wet
cock-and-bull story
crocodile tears
cry wolf
fourflusher
full of baloney
holler before it hurts
hot air
tinhorn

Generosity

chip in
give the shirt off one's back
give until it hurts
heart of gold
large-hearted
large-minded
open-handed
open-minded

Good Character

above suspicion
good as gold
good egg
good scout
heart of gold

Gratitude

half a loaf is better than none
thank one's lucky stars

Greed

itching palm
itchy palm
lick one's chops
on the take
pig out

Guilt

at fault
be to blame
blood on one's hands
caught with one's pants down
cop a plea
on one's chest
on one's head

Honesty

above suspicion
beyond reproach
call it as one sees it
children and fools speak the
    truth
clean hands
cross one's heart and hope to
    die
fair is fair
fair play
fair shake
give the devil his due
give the straight poop
go straight
heart-to-heart
honest as the day is long
honest injun
honest-to-goodness
lay all one's cards on the table
lay down one's cards
lay it on the line
lay one's cards on the table
let one's conscience be one's
    guide
level with
look in the eye
look in the face
make a clean breast of
man of his word
on one's honor
on the dead level
on the level
on the square
on the up and up
open-hearted
own up

place all one's cards on the table
place one's cards on the table
point of honor
put all one's cards on the table
put it on the line
put on the line
put one's cards on the table
put one's heart on one's sleeve
search one's heart
search one's soul
shoot from the hip
shoot straight
speak one's mind
speak out
speak up
square shooter
straight and narrow
straightforward
straight from the shoulder
straight out
straight shooter
talk turkey
tell it like it is
up front
woman of her word

Immorality

fall into sin

Indecency

off-color
off-colored

Ingratitude

bite the hand that feeds one
look a gift horse in the mouth

Inhumanity

heart of stone
in cold blood
reign of terror

Innocence

babe in the woods
dewy-eyed
wet behind the ears
wide-eyed

Insincerity

butter up
butter wouldn't melt in one's
    mouth
glad hand
go through the motions
left-handed
left-handed compliment
lip service
play to the gallery
two-faced

Mockery

make fun of
make light of
make little of
make sport of
poke fun at
pour cold water on
put down
send up
send-up

Propaganda

big lie

Prudery

bluenose
Mrs. Grundy
nice nelly
prim and proper
uptight

Punishment

do time
fix one's little red wagon
fix one's wagon
get it in the neck
get off easy
get one's lumps
go hard with
make an example of
pay for
put through hell
send up the river
take it out on
take one's lumps
tan one's hide
tar and feather
teach a lesson
throw away the key
throw the book at
walk the plank
wear stripes

Purloining

five-finger discount
make away with
make off with

Sanctimoniousness

butter wouldn't melt in one's
    mouth
holier-than-thou

Sincerity

actions speak louder than
    words
from the bottom of one's heart
from the heart
in earnest
in good faith
out front
so help me
so help me God
soul-searching
with all one's heart
with one's heart and soul

Slander

badmouth

Spirituality

get religion

Subversion/Sabotage

cut the ground from under
cut the ground out from under
double-cross
go back on
go over to the other side
play one false
poison-pen
rat on
sell down the river
sell out
stab in the back
tell on
throw a monkey wrench into
throw sand in the works
two-time

Swearing

curse out
swear a blue streak
swear like a drunken sailor
swear like a trooper
turn the air blue

Unfairness

below the belt
bum rap
hit below the belt
load the dice
stack the cards

Trust

take at one's word

Virtue

heart of gold
in the right
lily-white
pure as the driven snow
sweet as pie

Physical World

Acceptability

fit for consumption
fit for duty
fit for use
pass inspection

Accessibility

at hand
at one's elbow
at one's fingertips
in hand
off-the-peg
off-the-rack
off-the-shelf
open one's doors
open sesame
open the door
open up

Accuracy

close to home
close to the bone
come to the point
draw a bead on
draw blood
fill the bill
fit like a glove
get a fix on
have one pegged
hit the bull's-eye
hit the nail on the head
in effect
in fact
in point of fact
nose in
on a dime
on target
on the button
on the dot
on the mark
on the nose
right as rain
right on the button

right on the nose
smack-dab
straight as an arrow
touch a nerve

Adornment

best bib and tucker
deck out
dressed to kill
dressed to the nines
dressed to the teeth
gussy up
trick out
trick up

Assault

blitzkrieg
send in the troops
set the dogs on

Attractiveness

able to charm the birds from
the trees

bright as a button
bright as a new penny
cat's meow
cute as a bee's knee
cute as a bug's ear
cute as a button
cute trick
easy on the eyes
look like a million dollars
make one's mouth water
nice as can be
nice as pie
picture perfect
pretty as a picture
pretty enough to eat
smooth apple
spit and polish

Authenticity

honest-to-God
honest-to-goodness
real McCoy
real thing

Availability

for the asking
in season
in short supply

on deposit
on hand
on tap
open up
out of season
over-the-counter

Cold

cold as a mackerel
cold as ice
frozen stiff

Benefit

do one good
do one's heart good
in one's favor
on the cuff
on the house

Danger

lion's den
lion's mouth
sit on a bomb
sit on a hornet's nest
sit on a volcano
take one's life in one's hands

Blindness

blind as a bat
stone blind

Death

breathe one's last
cash in
cash in one's chips
die in one's boots
die off
die with one's boots on
drop dead
give up the ghost
go over to the other side
head for the last roundup

Clarity

clear as a bell
clear as day
clear as the nose on one's face
plain as the nose on one's face

kick off
kick the bucket
lie down and die

lie in state
meet one's maker
pass away
pass on
pop off
push daisies
push up daisies
roll over and die
spill one's guts
stone-cold dead
stone dead

out of order
out of practice
out of shape
out of whack
stone blind
stone deaf
worse for wear

Disappearance

die away
die off
fall away
fizzle out
gone with the wind
hell and gone
into thin air
make oneself scarce
vanishing point

Direction

as the crow flies
follow one's nose
from all sides
right and left
straight as an arrow
straight as the crow flies

Disability

blind as a bat
leak like a sieve
on the blink
on the fritz
out of commission
out of condition
out of kilter

Disaster

about one's ears
around one's ears
bite the dust
bottom drop out
bottom fall out
come a cropper
come to grief
cook one's goose

down the drain
ill-fated
lose one's shirt
on the rocks
pull down about one's ears
pull down around one's ears
pull the plug
pull the rug from under
throw a wet blanket on
throw cold water on
to hell and gone
wrack and ruin

Discard

flotsam and jetsam
pitch out
throw away
throw out

Disorganization

any which way
every which way
forty ways to Sunday
go haywire
mare's nest

Distress

between a rock and a hard
    place
hard sledding
hard up

Disturbance

big stink
make a scene
raise a fuss
raise a row
raise Cain
raise havoc
raise heck
raise hell
raise hob
raise Ned
raise ructions
raise the dead
raise the devil
raise the roof
tempest in a teapot

Domesticity

keep house

Dress

best bib and tucker
deck out
dressed to kill
dressed to the nines
dressed to the teeth
dressed up like Astor's pet horse
glad rags
look as if one has come out of a bandbox
Sunday best
Sunday go-to-meeting clothes

Drinking

bend an elbow
cocked
cockeyed
corked
drown one's sorrows
drown one's troubles
elbow-bending
fall off the wagon
feeling no pain
fried to the eyebrows
fried to the eyes
fried to the gills
fried to the hat
get one's brains fried
half in the bag
half seas over

have a bun on
have a glow on
have a load on
have a snootful
high as a kite
higher than a kite
hit the bottle
hit the sauce
hollow leg
hung over
in one's cups
knock back
liquored up
lit up
lit up like a Christmas tree
loaded
load on
looped
lubricated
off the sauce
off the wagon
oiled
on a toot
one for the road
one too many
pick-me-up
pie-eyed
soused to the gills
stewed to the gills
stiff as a goat
stiff as a plank
three sheets to the wind
tie one on
tight as a tick
under the table
wet one's whistle
wiped out

Enumeration

count heads
count noses

Explosion/ Explosiveness

blow sky high
go off like a rocket

Flatness

flat as a board
flat as a pancake

Food/Nourishment

done to a turn
eat like a bird
eat like a horse
eat out of house and home

eyes bigger than one's
    stomach
put on the feed bag
put on the nose bag
sling hash
stick to one's ribs
stick to the ribs
sweet tooth

Gaudiness

lit up like a Christmas tree
lit up like a church
lit up like a store window
lit up like Main Street
lit up like the sky
lit up like Times Square

Good Health

all better
feel like a million
fit as a fiddle
picture of health

Health

catch cold
catch one's death
come down with
feel like a million
fit as a fiddle
glow with health
hale and hearty
in condition
in shape
in the pink
in the pink of condition
in the pink of health
look oneself
picture of health

not long for
not long for this world
off one's feed
on one's last legs
one foot in the grave
pale around the gills
run a fever
run a temperature
run down
sick as a dog
take cold
take ill
take one's death of
take sick
the runs
the shakes
the touristas
the trots
throw up
throw up one's guts
toss one's cookies
under the weather

Husband

lord and master
old man

Illness

blue around the gills
catch cold
catch one's death of
green around the gills
lay up
Montezuma's revenge

Imitation

copycat
follow suit
monkey see, monkey do
take after

Impact

like a ton of bricks
plow into

Impediment

fly in the ointment
jam up

Liberation

at liberty
go scot-free
on the street

Livelihood

bread and butter
bread-and-butter
bring home the bacon
feather one's nest
hand out one's shingle
line one's nest
push a pen
push a pencil

Loss

kiss good-by
lose out
miss out
miss the boat
miss the bus
out the window

Luxury

eat high off the hog
eat high on the hog
eat one's cake and have it, too
fit for a king
have one's cake and eat it, too
high roller
high style
in style
in the lap of luxury
life of Riley
live high off the hog
live high on the hog
live in luxury
live of the fat of the land
on easy street
silk-stocking

Masculinity

all boy
hairy-chested
he-man
macho
musclebound

Medication

dope up
feeling no pain
hopped up

Misfortune

down on one's luck
out of luck

Money

cash on the barrelhead
cash on the line
cold cash
dead broke

fast buck
filthy lucre
flat broke
hard cash
have money to burn
in a hole
in arrears
in the black
in the chips
in the hole
in the money
in the red
made of money
make a mint
money to burn
on one's uppers
on the rims
out of one's own pocket
out-of-pocket
penny-pinching
penny-wise and pound-foolish
piece of change
pinch pennies
pony up
poor-mouth
purse strings
put the arm on
put the bite on
quick buck
red cent
red ink
rich as a lord
rich as Croesus
ride the gravy train
sock away
spend like a drunken sailor
stone broke
tight-fisted
tightwad

well-heeled
well-to-do
wherewithal

Mortality

at death's door
not long for this world
on one's last legs
one foot in the grave

Naturalness

in one's blood
in one's element
in the raw
in the rough

Need

in need
of necessity
rainy day

Nimbleness

light as a feather
light on one's feet
light-fingered
light-footed
light-handed

Nudity

birthday suit
in the altogether
in the buff
in the raw
naked as a jaybird
naked as the day one was
   born
stark naked
starkers
without a stitch

Operationalism

in circulation
in practice
in progress
in service
in the groove
in the works

off and running
off to the races
on duty
on one's way
on schedule
on the beam
on the job
on the march
on the move
take effect

Orderliness

apple-pie order
in a row
in order
in place
neat as a pin
square away
to rights

Overfullness

burst at the seams
burst one's seams

Physical Attributes: Negative

a face that only a mother
   could love
a face that would stop a clock
down-at-heel
homely as a hedge fence
ill-favored
pale around the gills
pale as a ghost
pale as death
skin and bones
white around the gills
white as a ghost
white as a sheet
yellow around the gills

Physical Attributes: Positive

bright as a button
light as a feather
neat as a pin
peaches-and-cream
pink as a baby's bottom
pretty as a picture
smooth as glass
smooth as silk
soft as silk

Physical Violence

beat the stuffing out of
cold cock
come to blows
draw and quarter
draw blood
hang a mouse on
knock one's block off
knock the daylights out of
knock the living daylights out
   of
knock the stuffing out of
lay a finger on
lay flat
lay waste
lift a hand
old one-two
pin one's ears back
punch out
punch up
raise a finger
raise a hand
rough stuff
rough up
round on
rub out
slap around
take apart
take a poke at
tan one's hide
tar and feather
tooth and nail
whale away at
within an inch of one's life
work over

Pokiness

hole-in-the-wall

Pregnancy

great with child
have one in the oven
in a family way
in the family way
knock up
on the pill
preggers
with child

Protection

bundle up
take under one's wing

Publicness

common coin
common knowledge
in public

in the limelight
in the public eye
open secret
out in the open
out of the closet
shout from the housetops
shout from the rooftops
show and tell

rack time
roll up the sidewalks
sack out
sack time
saw gourds
saw wood
sleep like a baby
sleep like a log
sleep the sleep of the dead
turn in

Reduction

mark down
scale down
taper off

Severity

beat into one's head
beat on
beat one's brains out
beat the stuffing out of
beat up on

Rest/Sleep

catch forty winks
catch one's breath
catch some Zs
conk out
cork off
dead to the world
get some shut-eye
go to bed with the chickens
hit the hay
hit the kip
hit the sack
in the arms of Morpheus
land of Nod

Sex

bag job
get into one's pants
get laid
get off
get one's ashes hauled
get one's oil changed
get one's rocks off
give head
go all the way

go down
go down on
have lead in one's pencil
hot for
lady-killer
lady's man
make a pass
make a pass at
make it with
make out
make-out artist
mess around with
play around
play doctor
play house
play the field
play with oneself
put out
roll in the hay
shack up
sleep around
sleep together
sleep with
swing both ways
switch-hit
switch-hitter
turn a trick

Subsistence

eat like a bird
eat like a horse
eat like a pig
hand-to-mouth
wolf down

Substitution

do duty for
fill one's shoes
in lieu of
in one's boots
in one's shoes
in one's stead
in place of
instead of
pinch-hit
speak for
step into one's shoes

Suffering

go through hell
go through the agonies of hell
go through the mill
go without
hard way
have a cross to bear
in the pits
lead a dog's life
living death
put through hell
put through the mill
put through the wringer
stew in one's own juice
sweat blood
sweat bullets
take one's lumps
take it on the chin
through hell and high water
vale of tears

Sustenance

bread and butter
bread-and-butter

Temperature

cold as a mackerel
cold as ice
colder than a mackerel
hot as hades
hot as hell
hot as the hinges of hell
hot enough to fry ice

Toughness

blood and guts
blood and thunder
hairy-chested
hard as nails
rough and tough
tough as nails
tough as they come

Unattractiveness

a face that only a mother
   could love
a face that would stop a clock
look like the wrath of God
look like the wreck of the
   Hesperus
ugly as sin
ugly duckling
ugly enough to tree a wolf

Unconsciousness

conk out
dead to the world
keel over
out cold
out like a light
pass out
pass out cold
zonked out

Understanding

comes the dawn
come to conclusions
come to one's senses
get it
get one's drift

get one's signals straight
get the general idea
get the idea
get the message
get the picture
get through one's head
get through one's skull
get through one's thick head
get through one's thick skull
get wise
get with it
give to understand
have one's number
know a thing or two about
know like a book
know like the back of one's
    hand
make head or tail of
make out
read between the lines
read one like a book
read one's mind
see daylight
see the daylight
see the light
sink in
take in

hold the bag
hold the sack
play into the hands of
scapegoat
take the rap
whipping boy

Weariness

bone tired
burn out
on one's last legs

Weather

rain buckets
rain cats and dogs
rain on
rain pitchforks
rained out

Victimization

at one's mercy
at the mercy of
clay pigeon
easy mark
fall guy

Wife

ball and chain
better half
little woman
old lady

Quality

Adequacy

no better than one should be
not anything to sneeze at
not bad
not half bad
not so bad
not too bad
nothing to sneeze at

Cheapness

dime-store
for a song
jerry-built

Clumsiness

all thumbs
bull in a china shop
fall all over oneself
ham-fisted
heavy-footed
heavy-handed
two left feet

Ambiguity

cut both ways
cut two ways
neither fish, flesh, nor fowl
neither fish nor fowl
neither here nor there

Commonplaceness

as usual
at every turn
common as an old shoe
common as mud
dime a dozen
run-of-the-mill
run-of-the-mine

Comparison

have nothing on
hold a candle to
next to
not have anything on
nothing like
put to shame
vis-à-vis

Conciseness

in a nutshell
in a word
in brief
in short
in so many words
long and the short of it
short and sweet
short-spoken

Decline

for the worse
from bad to worse
go down
go downhill
go from bad to worse
go into a nose dive
go to hell
go to hell in a hand basket
go to pot
go to seed
go to the devil
go to the dogs
go to wrack and ruin
not up to par
not up to scratch
not up to snuff
on the skids
on the wane
seen better days
take a turn for the worse
waste away
wind down
wither on the vine

Difference

horse of another color
horse of a different color
poles apart
put a different light on
put into a different light
see in a different light
whole new ball game

Disadvantage

get the worst of
have two strikes against one
in the street
leave without a leg to stand on
over a barrel
over the barrel
put in a bad light
short end
short end of the stick
sticky end of the stick
wrong side of the tracks

Easiness/Ease

as easy as ABC
as easy as falling off a log
as easy as pie
as easy as rolling off a log
as easy as shooting fish in a
  barrel
as easy as taking candy from a
  baby
breeze along
breeze by
breeze through
comfortable as an old shoe
common as an old shoe
duck soup
easy does it
easy street
lead-pipe cinch
line of least resistance

make oneself at home
no sweat
piece of cake
primrose path
think nothing of
toss off
travel light
waltz through
win in a breeze
win in a walk

Elite

cream of the crop
crème de la crème
haut monde

Emancipation

free as a bird
free as a butterfly
free as the breeze
free as the wind
get the monkey off one's back

Error

all wet
get off on the wrong foot
ill-advised
in the wrong
jump the track
lead astray
load of hooey
louse up
miss by a mile
off base
off the beam
out in left field
pull a boner
put one's foot in it
put one's foot in one's mouth
put one's money on a
  scratched horse
slip of the lip
slip of the pen
slip of the pencil
slip of the tongue
slip up
slip-up
start off on the wrong foot
stray from the beaten path
stray from the straight and
  narrow
talk through one's hat

burn out
burn the candle at both ends
dead in one's tracks
dead on one's feet
dead tired
drop by the wayside
knock oneself out
knocked out
limp as a dishrag
limp as a rag
limp as a wet noodle
milk dry
out of breath
out of gas
out of it
out of steam
peter out
played out
run into the ground
run out
run ragged
shoot one's bolt
shoot one's load
sick and tired
sick to death
strung out
tire out
wear away
wear down
wear on
wear out
wear out one's welcome
wiped out
wrung out

Exhaustion

blow out
blue in the face

Experience

a burnt child dreads the fire
dry behind the ears
get the feel of
go through
have been around
learn one's lesson
learn one's way around
learn the hard way
learn the ropes
live and learn
sadder but wiser
school of hard knocks
teach the ropes
tricks of the trade
under one's belt

Failure

about one's ears
around one's ears
come to naught
come to nothing
conk out
cop out
down-and-out
down-at-heel
down the drain
down the toilet
down the tube
draw a blank
drop by the wayside
fall by the wayside
fall down
fall down on the job
fall flat
fizzle out
go down the drain
go down the tubes
go over like a lead balloon
go under
hit an all-time low
hit bottom
in vain
lay a bomb
lay an egg
lose ground
memento mori
no soap
on the skids
pull a Brodie
screw up
strike out
two-time loser
wash out

Familiarity

after one's own heart
close to home
old saw
old story
stamping ground

Fastidiousness

just so

Favor

fair-haired boy
in good
in one's good graces
in one's good books
on one's good side
take kindly to

Fitting Behavior

act one's age
be one's age
brownie points
earn brownie points
mind one's manners
mind one's p's and q's
on one's good behavior
put one's best foot forward

Freedom

at liberty
break loose
carte blanche
free as a bird
free hand
free rein
get away with murder
on the loose
open season
open-ended
rid of
sky's the limit
take liberties
turn loose

Freedom of Choice

at whim
at will
blank check
free hand
give free rein
pick and choose
write one's own ticket

Fullness

full as a fiddle
full as a goat
full as a goose
full as a lord
full as a tick
full to bursting
full to the brim

Importance

big frog in a little pond
big frog in a small pond
big time
big-time
blockbuster
brass hat
class act
cock of the walk
double in brass
go down in history
go down in the record books
go down in the records
last of the big-time spenders
last of the red-hot lovers
legend in one's own time
life of the party
little frog in a big pond
man of parts
movers and shakers
nothing to sneeze at
number one
numero uno

red-letter day
small frog in a big pond
that ain't hay
top banana
top dog
visiting fireman

Improvement

do one good
for the better
get back on one's feet
go one better
iron out
look up
make over
on the mend
pull into shape
pull oneself together
pull oneself up by one's
    bootstraps
pull oneself up by the
    bootstraps
put into shape
put one's house in order
put to rights
raise one's sights
refine on
regain one's feet
shape up
spruce up
step in the right direction
straighten out
straighten up and fly right

touch up
tune up
wear off
whip into shape

out of line
out of one's element
out of order
out of place
out of step
out of sync
out of tune
square peg
square peg in a round hole

Inaccuracy

away out in left field
in left field
off in left field
out in left field
wide of the mark

Inconsequentiality

chicken feed
don't make no never-mind
for the birds
make no never-mind
no matter
not worth a cent
not worth a damn
not worth a dime
not worth a tinker's damn
one-horse
pip-squeak
small potatoes
small-time

Inadequacy

half-baked
half-cocked
half-cooked
like a fish out of water
no bargain
no prize
plenty of nothing

Increase

jack up
mark up

Inappropriateness

out of character
out of keeping

pile up
soup up
step up

Ineptitude

all thumbs
blind leading the blind
left-handed
not let the left hand know
    what the right hand is doing

Inexperience

not dry behind the ears
wet behind the ears

Inferiority

dime-a-dozen
dime-store
hand-me-down
other side of the tracks
piss-poor
poor-man's

reach-me-down
second best
second class
small-time
take the booby prize
ticky-tacky
two-bit
wrong side of the tracks

Instability

catch-as-catch-can
house of cards
in a bad way
jump around
thrown together
up in the air

Intensity

hot and heavy
hot up
like crazy
like mad
red-hot
stepped-up

Margin

by a hair
by a long shot
by a mile
by a nose
by a thread
by a whisker
by the seat of one's pants
by the seat of the pants
margin for error

Mediocrity

fair-to-middling
no ball of fire
no bargain
no great shakes
no prize
not so hot
nothing to brag about
nothing to write home about
so-so

Misjudgment

bark up the wrong tree
bet on the wrong horse
lead astray
lose sight of
lose track
not see beyond the end of
  one's nose
off the track
out in left field
throw the baby out with the
  bath water

Moderation

middle-of-the-road
tone down

Normalcy

boy next door
boys will be boys
girl next door
par for the course
up to par
up to scratch
up to snuff
up to the mark

Nuisance

fly in the ointment
pain in the neck
pain in the rear end
thorn in one's flesh
thorn in one's side

Omission

leave out
leave out of account
reckon without
rule out
skip it
skip over

Obstacle

stone wall
stumbling block

Obviousness

go without saying
hit between the eyes
in evidence
plain as day
plain as the nose on one's face
stare one in the face
stick out like a sore thumb
under one's nose
under one's very nose

Organization

apple-pie order
get it all together
get it on
get one's act together
line up
set one's house in order
set one straight
set to rights
settle one's affairs

Originality

don't make them like that any
   more
one and only
one in a million
one of a kind
sui generis
threw away the mold

Outward Appearance

on the face of it
on the surface

right guy
rotten egg
straight arrow
tough guy
wet blanket
wise guy
wiseacre
wisenheimer

Perilous Situation

between life and death
between Scylla and Charybdis
between the devil and the
   deep blue sea
between the devil you know
   and the devil you don't
   know
between two fires
between two stools
beyond one's depth
bite off more than one can
   chew
life-and-death

Pointlessness

cry over spilled milk
cry over spilt milk
no use
no use crying over spilled milk
no use crying over spilt milk
of no avail
to no avail
waste one's breath
wild-goose chase

Personality

crepehanger
good egg
good scout
holy terror
party pooper
regular fellow
regular guy

Pomposity

have one's nose stuck in the
   air
high-and-mighty
high-flown
high-flying
high-sounding
high-toned

highfalutin
full of hot air
jumped-up
know-it-all
put on airs
put on the dog
put on the ritz
queen it
stuck-up
stuffed shirt
too big for one's boots
too big for one's breeches
too big for one's britches

Poor Judgment

bark up the wrong tree
bet on the wrong horse
off the track

Popularity

in demand
rate with

Praise

get a pat on the back
give a pat on the back
nice going
nice work

Priority

first and foremost
first and last
first come, first served
first off
first things first
have other fish to fry
have the cart before the horse
in the first place
last but not least
number one
order of the day
put the cart before the horse
right of way
take a back seat
to the fore

Privacy

behind closed doors
in private
keep it in the family
keep mum

Privilege

best of both worlds
eat one's cake and have it, too

Quality

class act
cut above
fair-to-middling
make the difference
of the first order
one and only
one of the best
stand out
top of the line
top-drawer
top-hole
topnotch

Realistic Assessment

beggars can't be choosers
black-and-white
bottom line
cannot make a silk purse out
of a sow's ear
cannot make bricks without
straw
it takes what it takes

name of the game
play it as it lays
read one like a book
take at face value
where there's smoke there's
fire

Reliability

as good as one's promise
as good as one's word
exception proves the rule
hold good
stand one in good stead
straight from the horse's
mouth
swear by

Repellency

burn out
off-putting
stick in one's craw
stick in one's crop
stick in one's gizzard

Replaceableness

not the only fish in the ocean
not the only fish in the sea
not the only pebble on the
  beach

Routine

cut and dried
matter-of-course

Reservation

as it were
at the same time
have second thoughts
much less
on condition

Security

better safe than sorry
home free
in the clear
safe and sound
safety in numbers
security blanket

Reticence

cat has one's tongue
hide one's light under a bushel
hold back
hold one's peace
man of few words
shrinking violet
tight-lipped
tight-mouthed

Selectiveness

hit the high points
touch the high points
pick over
separate the men from the
  boys
separate the wheat from the
  chaff
weed out

Sensibleness

common touch
down-to-earth
have a good head on one's
   shoulders
old-shoe
within reason

Situation

fine how-do-you-do
fine how-d'ya-do
fine kettle of fish
how the land lies
how the wind blows
kettle of fish
lay of the land
nice how-do-you-do
pretty kettle of fish

Similarity

birds of a feather
chip off the old block
follow in one's footsteps
in one's footsteps
kindred souls
kindred spirits
like father, like son
look-alike
much of a muchness
one and the same
six of one, half-dozen of the
   other
spit and image
spitting image

Slowness

lead-footed
like a bump on a log
slow as molasses
slow as molasses flowing
   uphill in January
slow on the draw
slow on the uptake
snail's pace

Simplicity

boil down
open-and-shut
simple as pie

Sobriety

clear as a bell
cold sober
on the wagon
on the water wagon
sober as a buck shad

sober as a church
sober as a deacon
sober as a judge
sober as a shoemaker
take the pledge

Social Status

ragtag
ragtag and bobtail
rank and file
riffraff
tag, rag, and bobtail

Stability

feet on the ground
find one's way
keep one's feet
keep one's feet on the ground
keep one's head
find oneself
level off
level out
on an even keel
put down roots
settle down
steady as a rock
sure-footed
take root
take shape

Spontaneity

by ear
fly blind
fly by the seat of one's pants
obiter dictum
off the cuff
off the top of one's head
off-the-cuff
on the spur of the moment
open-ended
play by ear
spur-of-the-moment
take a notion
wing it

Status

all walks of life
cut above
fair-to-middling
first-class
one and only
upper crust
walk of life

Strength

beef up
hold up
pack a punch
pack a wallop
red-blooded
strength of ten men
strong as a bull
strong as an ox
two-fisted

Superfluousness/ Superabundance

alive with
carry coals to Newcastle
it never rains but it pours
lousy with
no end to

Superiority

down one's nose
have it all over
have it over
have nothing on
have one's nose stuck in the
     air
head and shoulders above
high-hat
lord it over
make look sick
off the top shelf
on one's high horse
on top
out in front
outclass
outmatch
prima inter pares
right side of the tracks
rise above
rise to the occasion
run circles around
run rings around
salt of the earth

Style

newfangled
old hat
old-fangled
old-fashioned
old-time
old-timey
out of it
out-of-date
up-to-date
up-to-the-minute
with it

Superficiality

lick and a promise
skin deep

stand head and shoulders
   above
to the king's taste
to the queen's taste
turn up one's nose at

Superlativeness

out of sight
out of this world
the bee's knees
the berries
the cat's pajamas
the greatest
the nuts
the ticket

Suspicion/ Suspiciousness

bad vibes
bad vibrations
queer as a three-dollar bill
smell a rat
smell fishy
smell smoke
smell to high heaven
stink to high heaven

Tentativeness

feel one's way

Triteness

cornball
Mickey Mouse
old chestnut
old hat
rinky-dink
war horse
wear thin

Triviality

nitpick
split hairs

Trouble

get in Dutch
get in hot water
in a jam

in a spot
in deep water
in Dutch
in hot water
in the soup
on the rocks
on the skids
on the spot
open up a can of worms
put to it
run afoul of
run foul of
start something
stir up a hornet's nest

Uniqueness

one-shot
sui generis

Unity

as one man
close ranks

Unavailability

out of print
out of stock

Undesirability

need like a hole in the head
need like one needs a hole in
   the head

Unpleasant Experience

bad trip
body blow
burn one's fingers
cold turkey
hell on wheels
pain in the neck
rotten egg
royal pain
royal pain in the neck
the pits
thumb in the eye

Unpleasant Personality

bad actor
bad egg
bad news
cold fish
crepehanger
heart of stone
hell on wheels
killjoy
pain in the neck
party pooper
poor fish
royal pain
royal pain in the neck
spoilsport

Unreliability

fair-weather friend
hanging fire
here today, gone tomorrow
hit-and-miss
hit-or-miss
up in the air

Unsettledness

betwixt and between

Unpleasant Reality

bad news
bad scene
body blow
cold turkey
facts of life
hell of a note
honeymoon is over
in the face of
rum go

Urgency

at all costs
beg, borrow, or steal
build a fire under
cry for
cry out for
down to the wire
drop everything
fast and furious
on short notice
run scared

Vagueness

after a fashion
fuzzy around the edges
fuzzy-minded
in a kind of way
in a sense
in a sort of way
in a way
kind of

Waste

fritter away
go begging
go by the board
go down the drain
go down the tubes
go to waste
time-consuming

Vulnerability

at one's mercy
at the mercy of
cards stacked against one
feet of clay
flatfooted
lay oneself open
leave oneself open
leave oneself wide open
line of fire
not a leg to stand on
off balance
off base
off guard
sitting duck
soft touch
thin-skinned

Weakness

lame duck
namby-pamby
on one's last legs
water down
weak in the knees
weak sister
weak-kneed
wishy-washy

Worsening

add fuel to the fire
add fuel to the flames
add insult to injury
jump from the frying pan into
   the fire
leap from the frying pan into
   the fire

open up a new can of worms
out of the frying pan into the
fire

Worthiness

blessing in disguise
diamond in the rough
prince among men
without price
worth a fortune
worth a mint
worth one's weight in gold

Relationship

Admiration

look up to
put on a pedestal
take a shine to

right on
same here
see eye to eye
see fit
settle for
silence gives consent
string along

Agreement

ain't it the truth
bet one's boots
come to terms
common ground
get on
I'll drink to that
in tune
like-minded
meeting of minds
O.K.
okey-doke
okle-dokle

Association

go around together
go around with
go steady
hand-in-hand
hook up
in touch
in tow
keep company
keep company with
on the bandwagon
pair off

139

pair up
pal around
shoulder to shoulder
side by side

Attachment

cling to one's apron strings
cling to one's mother's apron
    strings
clinging vine

Circumstance

in the circumstances
in the light of
in view of
just the same
under the circumstances

Close Surveillance

breathe down one's neck
get the goods on
keep an eye on

Competition/ Competitiveness

dog-eat-dog
get the best of
get the better of
get the jump on
get the worst of
give as good as one gets
go one better
jockey for position
keep up with the Joneses
last word
nose out
one up
one-upmanship
pit against
rat race
steal one's thunder
steal the show
steal the spotlight
tug of war

Conflict

at cross purposes
at loggerheads
at odds
at swords' points
cross swords
fight to the finish
fight tooth and nail
go at it

go at it hammer and tongs
go at it tooth and nail
have it out
run-in

throw in one's face
throw in one's teeth
to one's face
toe-to-toe

Conformity

according to Hoyle
against the current
against the grain
fall in
fall in with
in step

Cooperation

compare notes
get together
give and take
go all the way
go halfway
go halfway to meet one
hand and glove
hand in glove
hand-in-hand
hang together
join forces
join hands
join ranks
many hands make light work
on one's good behavior
play ball
play ball with
play the game
pull together
put heads together
quid pro quo
scratch one's back
shoulder to shoulder
team effort

Confrontation

eyeball to eyeball
face to face
fly in the face of
fly in the teeth of
in one's face
lock horns
mix it up
nose to nose
put it to one
run against
sock it to
spar with
square off
take on

Dependence

bank on
fall back on
hinge on
lean on
set great store by
set store by
tied to one's apron strings
tied to one's mother's apron
   strings

Identity

after one's own heart
birds of a feather
like father, like son
like two peas in a pod
two of a kind

Intimacy

heart-to-heart
like two peas in a pod
man-to-man
one-on-one
thick as thieves
under one's skin
woman-to-woman

Friendliness

get on
glad-hand
hail-fellow-well-met
hit it off
make friends with
one of the boys
open one's doors to
palsy-walsy
put out the welcome mat
rub elbows
rub shoulders
welcome with open arms

Kinship

birds of a feather
birds of a feather flock
   together
chip off the old block
close-knit
flesh-and-blood
kith and kin
like father, like son
near and dear

under the skin
work the same side of the
    street

Marriage

get hitched
jump the hurdle
pop the question
rob the cradle
take the plunge
tie the knot

Moral Support

behind one
behind one all the way
behind one one-hundred
    percent

Rank

big time
first among equals
number one
numero uno

Reciprocity

in kind
in return
one hand washes the other
quid pro quo
return the compliment
tit for tat
you scratch my back and I'll
    scratch yours

Reconciliation

bury the ax
bury the hatchet
bury the tomahawk
kiss and make up
make peace
make up
water over the dam
water under the bridge

Remoteness

far cry
in a world by oneself
in a world of one's own
in one's own little world
ivory tower

keep a distance
keep at a distance
keep at arm's length
keep one's distance
keep to oneself
out of the picture
out of touch
out-of-the-way

Sharing

fifty-fifty
give away
give of oneself
go halves
in common
in the same boat
parcel out
partake of
people-to-people
piece of the action
piece out
share and share alike
split the difference

Size / Movement

Conclusion

bitter end
bring down the curtain
bring up the rear
call it quits
cut and dried
payoff
tag end
tail end

Degree

and then some
at the most
by half
by leaps and bounds
by the seat of one's pants
by the seat of the pants
far and away

few and far between
first-class
for love or money
for the most part
in the least
in the slightest
less and less
more and more
more or less
not a little
quite a bit
quite a little
short of
to a degree

Departure

blow the joint
clear out
cut and run

cut for
cut out
get away
get lost
go bye-bye
head out
light out
make sail
pack off
peel off
pull away
pull stakes
pull up stakes
push off
push on
put out to sea
put to sea
run along
run off
ship out
shove off
show a clean pair of heels
take a powder
take leave of
take off
take one's leave of
up stakes
vote with one's feet
walk out
walk out on

come around
come into one's own
come into the picture
come of age
come true
come up in the world
drag oneself up by the
    bootstraps
get a leg up

Exactness

---

chapter and verse
line for line
word for word

Development

---

come a long way
come about

Exaggeration

---

blow up
cock-and-bull story
far-fetched
fish story
gild the lily
hype up
lay it on thick
lay it on with a trowel
line of bull
load of hooey
make a big thing of
make a mountain out of a
    molehill

make something of
paint the lily
pour it on
put it on thick
song and dance
spread it on thick
strain a point
stretch a point
tall story
tall tale
tall talk
tart up

Example

for instance
pacemaking
pacesetting
set an example
set the pace
such as

Extravagance

cost an arm and a leg
high, wide, and handsome
high-flying
in a big way
jazz up

pull out all the stops
razzle-dazzle
razzmatazz

Extremity/Extremism

bitter end
deep end
deep water
down to the wire
drive to the wall
end of one's rope
end of one's tether
end of the line
end of the road
far-fetched
far-out
farthest thing from one's mind
fit to burst
fit to die
fit to kill
for love or money
go off the deep end
go to any length
hang by a hair
hang by a thread
have one's back against the wall
have one's back to the wall
in extremis
in the nick of time
just in time
last ditch
last-ditch attempt

last-ditch effort
last-ditch stand
last gasp
last straw
nick of time
nothing short of
off the deep end
on one's uppers
sky-high
straw that breaks the camel's
   back
string out
to a fault
to pieces
to the bitter end
to the bone
way out
way out in left field

make a beeline for
make a run for it
make for
make haste
make it snappy
make off
make time
make tracks
move it
move one's carcass
move one's tail
off in a flash
off like a flash
on the fly
on the run
on the wing
plunge ahead
right away
right now
right off
shake a leg
slap together
speed up
step lively
step on it
step on the gas
straightaway

Generality

at every turn
in any case
in any event
in general
on the whole

Inactivity

off-season
on the back burner
on the bench
on the shelf
stay put

Hurry

bum's rush
burn up the road

stay-at-home
stick-in-the-mud

Limitation

at most
within bounds

Miscellany

and so forth
and then some
bits and pieces
flotsam and jetsam
odds and ends
tag ends
what have you
what not

Narrow Margin

by a hair
by a nose
by a whisker
by the seat of one's pants
miss is as good as a mile

narrow escape
narrow squeak
near miss
neck and neck
nip and tuck
on the line
sneak by
split second
squeak by
squeak through
under the wire
wing and a prayer
within an ace of
within an inch of

Populousness

alive with
crawling with

Proportion

lion's share

Quantity

hand-over-fist
not a few
quite a few
quite a number
umpty-ump
without number

sawed-off
skinny as a rail
thin as a dime
thin as a rail
thin as a reed
thin as a wafer
to scale
tub of lard

Reinforcement

for good measure

Size

big as a house
big as all outdoors
big as life
big as life and twice as natural
bigger than a bread box
bigger than life
knee-high
knee-high to a duck
knee-high to a grasshopper
knee-high to a mosquito
large as life
long drink of water
pint-size
pint-sized
pip-squeak

Speed

get a hustle on
get a move on
get a wiggle on
get the lead out
get the lead out of one's pants
give her the gas
give her the gun
give it the gas
give it the gun
go like a bat out of hell
go like a house afire
go like sixty
gun it
hand-over-fist
hell-for-leather
hightail it
hop to it
hotfoot it
house afire
house on fire
immediately, if not sooner
in a jiff
in a jiffy
in nothing flat

in no time
in no time flat
in short order
in two shakes
in two shakes of a lamb's tail
lay rubber
leg it
less than no time
lickety-split
like a bat out of hell
like a house afire
like a shot
like a streak
like a streak of greased
    lightning
like a streak of lightning
like greased lightning
like 60
like sixty
line out
quick as a flash
quick as a fox
quick as a snake
quick as a snap
quick as a wink
quick as dust
quick as greased lightning
quick as lightning
quick on the draw
quick on the trigger
tear around

Sufficiency

little enough
little goes a long way
more than one bargained for
more than one can shake a
    stick at
more the merrier
no end of
up to par
up to scratch
up to snuff
up to the mark

Summary

roundup
rundown
say in so many words
sum total
sum up
the long and the short of it

Thoroughness

every inch
go down the line
high and low
inside and out
inside out
top to bottom

Universality

at every turn
common touch
down to earth
in all creation
on the lips of
under the sun

change of pace
mixed bag
mixed blessing
ring changes on
ring the changes
this and that
this, that, and the other
variety is the spice of life

Variety

all kinds of
all manner of
all sorts of
all work and no play makes
  Jack a dull boy

Vestige

hide nor hair
hide or hair
neither hide nor hair

Time / Space

Abruptness

bolt from the blue
in one's tracks
like a ton of bricks
off the bat
out from nowhere
out of a blue sky
out of a clear blue sky
out of a clear sky
out of nowhere
out of the blue
plunk down
pop up
right off the bat
short shrift
start off with a bang
strike all of a heap

Actuality

fact is
for real
here and now
in black and white
in fact
in name only
matter of fact
matter of record

Addition

in the bargain
into the bargain
on the side
over and above

Age

act one's age
along in years
babe in arms
be one's age
come of age
long in the tooth
no spring chicken
not what one used to be
of a certain age
older than Methuselah
older than the hills
on in years
one foot in the grave
over age
over the hill
prime of life
salad days
second childhood
spring chicken

Beginning

from scratch
ground floor
here goes
here goes nothing
jumping-off place
jumping-off point
ring up the curtain
scratch the surface
set about
set forth
set forward
set in
set in motion
set off
set out
set sail
set the ball rolling
set the stage
start from scratch
start in
stepping-off place

Arrival

blow in
breeze in
pull in
roll around
roll in
roll up

Completeness/ Completion

across the board
bag and baggage
bar none
beat the band
beat the bushes
by all manner of means
by all means

by all odds
by heart
come full circle
coming and going
down the line
drop a stitch
dyed-in-the-wool
each and every
en masse
every man jack
every which way
for all the world
forty ways to Sunday
from stem to stern
from the ground up
get the works
go whole hog
going and coming
hands down
head over heels
head to toe
heart and soul
hook, line, and sinker
in one piece
in the round
in toto
kit and caboodle
length and breadth
limb from limb
living daylights
lock, stock, and barrel
no end
of a piece
out-and-out
part and parcel
polish off
signed, sealed, and delivered
six ways to Sunday
the works

through and through
to a man
to the best of one's knowledge
to the full
to the hilt
to the nth degree
to the teeth
top off
up and down
up one side and down the
    other
up to one's chin
up to one's eyebrows
up to one's neck
up to the chin in
up to the eyebrows in
up to the hilt
up to the neck in
up to there
whole ball of wax
whole show
wrap it up
wrap up
wrap-up

Confinement

behind bars
hedge about
hedge in
hem in
shut in
snow in

Distance

as the crow flies
far and near
far and wide
hither and yon

Doom

beginning of the end
death knell
gone goose
handwriting on the wall
kiss of death

Equivalence

by the same token

Equivocation

as it were
at the same time
beat about the bush
beat around the bush

blow hot and cold
hem and haw
no doubt
of a sort
of sorts
on approval
on one hand
on the other hand
play with words
sit on the fence
so to speak
that is to say
that's to say
then again
think better of
weasel around
weasel words

Eventuality

in any case
in any event
in case
in the long run

Extension

branch off
farm out

Fate

beginning of the end
in the lap of the gods
it's all in the cards
it's not in the cards
on the knees of the gods

Foreshadowing

in the air
in the wind

Frequency

at all hours
at times
every now and again
every now and then
every once in a while
every so often
every time one turns around
less and less
more and more
more often than not
on an average
on occasion
on the average
once in a blue moon
once in a while
year in, year out
year-round

Finality

at last
at length
at long last
bottom line
bottom out
breathe one's last
bring down the curtain
call it a day
case closed
once and for all
once for all
that's that
then and there

Forbiddance

off limits
out-of-bounds

Future

in store
lay away
lay by

one of these days
some one of these days
sooner or later
straw in the wind

give pause
hang back

Good Fortune

as luck would have it
born with a silver spoon in
    one's mouth
luck of the Irish
luck out
lucky in love
stroke of luck
when one's ship comes in

Haphazardness

catch-as-catch-can

Hesitation

as it were
at the same time
far be it from me

Hindsight

back-seat driver
Monday-morning
    quarterback
second-guess
second-guesser

Idleness

fritter away
hang around
lay about
lay around
layabout
lazy bones
lie about
lie around
lounge lizard
on the street
pass the time of day
twiddle one's thumbs
while away

Immediacy

at sight
at the drop of a hat
just now
on the heels of
on the spot
straight off
straightaway
upon the heels of

Imminence

around the corner
close at hand
close to hand
near at hand
on the tip of one's tongue
on the verge
on the way

Impermanence

days are numbered
flash in the pan

Inevitability

boys will be boys
handwriting on the wall
in the cards
sure as shooting

Irregularity

hit-and-miss
hit-or-miss
off-again, on-again
off-and-on
on-again, off-again
on-and-off
out of turn
stop-and-go

Likelihood

never in a million years
never in all one's born days
never in one's wildest dreams

Location

neck of the woods

Occupancy

move in

Newness

at first blush
at first glance
at first sight
Johnny-come-lately
just off the boat
newfangled
off the boat
red-hot

Occurrence

come about
come by
come by honestly
come by naturally
come one's way
come to pass
come up
crop up
every now and again
every now and then
every once in a while
every so often
go down
take place

Occasionalness

every now and again
every now and then
every so often
from time to time
now and again
now and then

Past

back in the dark ages
before one's time
hark back
horse-and-buggy era
in the old days
once upon a time

used to be
way back when
when Hector was a pup
when the world was young

Perpetuity/ Permanence

day and night
day in, day out
for good
for good and all
for keeps
from now till doomsday
from now until doomsday
from way back
night and day
on end
round-the-clock
till hell freezes over
until hell freezes over
until the cows come home
until the moon turns to green
    cheese
when hell freezes over
world without end
year in, year out

Postponement

give a raincheck
let ride
on a back burner
on the back burner
period of grace
put on hold
put on ice
put off
put over
take a rain check

The Present

here and now
on-the-scene
on-the-spot
present-day

Punctuality

on the dot
on the minute
on the nose
on time

Randomness

every which way
here and there
hither and thither
hit-and-miss
hit-or-miss
hither and yon
this way and that
helter-skelter

Rarity

few and far between
off the beaten track
once in a blue moon
once in a lifetime
once in a while
one for the books
one in a million
oner
one of a kind
out of the ordinary
scarce as hen's teeth

Repetition

come again
over again
over and over

repeat oneself
time after time
time and again
time and time again

Separation

break up
divvy up
part company
parting of the ways
set apart
set aside
set by
split up

Serendipity

by chance
by happenstance
by a quirk of fate
by a stroke of luck
as luck would have it
by a twist of fate

Seriousness

all kidding aside
dead serious
for real
heavy weather
heavy-duty
mean business
no fooling
no joke
no kidding
no laughing matter
play for keeps
play for real
sober-sided
sobersides
spoilsport
straight face
straight-faced

Temporariness

blow over
for the nonce
for the time being

Termination

call a halt
case closed
curtains
call it a day
cut it out
death knell
deep-six
end of the line
end of the road
for good
for keeps
game is up
give the ax to
give the old heave ho
have done with
hold it
knock it off
knock off
leave off
make an end to
no longer
null and void
over and done with
over and out
over with
pack in
pack it in
pull up short
put a stop to
put an end to
put the kibosh on
ring down the curtain
shoot down
shut down
shut off
snuff out
stop cold
stop cold in one's tracks
stop dead
stop dead in one's tracks
swear off
wind up

Termination of Waiting

at last
at length
at long last

Time

against the clock
against time
ahead of time
all at once
all of a sudden
around the clock
at once
at the drop of a hat
bright and early
by and by
close at hand
come the dawn
come the millennium
coon's age
day and night
day in, day out
dog's age
down to the wire
early bird catches the worm
for the nonce
for the time being
forever and a day
here and now
in a while

in the long run
in time
latter-day
long haul
long pull
long range
moment by moment
month of Sundays
nowadays
now and again
now and then
of late
put back the clock
shank of the evening
short haul
short-range
so far
the good old days
thus far
to date
turn back the clock
until hell freezes over
up to now
up to the minute

Transience

blow over
days are numbered
die away
die down
die off
die on the vine
fade away

flash in the pan
fly-by-night
here today, gone tomorrow
in passing

Usualness

business as usual
go about one's business

go on about one's own
    business
in the line of duty
in the main
in practice
more of the same
more often than not
most always
most of the time
nothing new under the sun
nothing out of the ordinary
par for the course
on the whole
strictly routine

Index